Read Real NIHONGO

Japanese texts for intermediate learners

Japan Today and How It Got This Way

にほん　ろんてん
日本の論点

James M. Vardaman

ジェームス・M・バーダマン

Yvonne Chang＝translator

やく
イヴォンヌ・チャング＝訳

IBCパブリッシング

装　　帧＝見増 勇介、関屋 晶子(ym design)
翻訳協力＝ Matt Treyvaud

About the *Read Real NIHONGO* Series

Reading Sets You Free

The difficulty of reading Japanese is perhaps the greatest obstacle to the speedy mastery of the language. A highly motivated English speaker who wants to make rapid progress in a major European language such as Spanish, French or German need only acquire a grasp of the grammar and a smattering of vocabulary to become able to at least attempt to read a book. Thanks to a common alphabet, they can instantly identify every word on the page, locate them in a dictionary, and figure out—more or less—what is going on.

With Japanese, however, *kanji* ideograms make it infinitely harder to make the jump from reading with guidance from a teacher to reading freely by oneself. The chasm dividing the short example sentences of textbooks from the more intellectually rewarding world of real-world books and articles can appear unbridgeable. Japanese—to borrow Nassim Taleb's phrase—is an "Extremistan" language. *Either* you master two thousand *kanji* characters with their various readings to achieve breakthrough reading proficiency and the capacity for self-study *or* you fail to memorize enough *kanji*, your morale collapses, and you retire, tired of floating in a limbo of semi-literacy. At a certain point, Japanese is all or nothing, win or lose, put up or shut up.

The benefits of staying the course and acquiring the ability to read independently are, of course, enormous.

Firstly, acquiring the ability to study by yourself without needing a teacher increases the absolute number of hours that you can study from "classroom time only" to "as long as you want." If there is any truth to the theories about 10,000 hours of practice being needed to master any skill, then clearly the ability to log more hours of Japanese self-study has got to be a major competitive advantage.

Secondly, exposure to longer texts means that your Japanese input rises in simple quantitative terms. More Japanese *going into* your head means that, necessarily, more Japanese *stays in* your head! As well as retaining more words and idioms, you will also start to develop greater mental stamina. You will get accustomed to digesting Japanese in real-life "adult" portions rather than the child-sized portions you were used to in the classroom.

Thirdly, reading will help you develop tolerance for complexity as you start using context to help you figure things out for yourself. When reading a book, the process goes something like this: You read a sentence; should you fail to understand it first time, you read it again. Should it still not make sense to you, you can go onto the next sentence and use the meaning of that one to "reverse-engineer" the meaning of its predecessor, and so on. By doing this, you will become self-reliant, pragmatic and—this is significant—able to put up with gaps in your understanding without panicking, because you know they are only temporary. You will morph into a woodsman of language, able to live off the land, however it may be.

That is the main purpose of the *Read Real NIHONGO* series: to propel you across the chasm that separates those who read Japanese from those who cannot.

Furigana the Equalizer

Bilingual books have been popular in Japan since the 1990s. Over time, they have grown more sophisticated, adding features like comprehensive page-by-page glossaries, illustrations and online audio. What makes the *Read Real NIHONGO* series—a relative latecomer to the scene—special?

It all comes down to *furigana*. This is the first ever series of bilingual books to include *furigana* superscript above every single *kanji* word in the text. Commonly used in children's books in Japan, *furigana* is a tried-and-tested, non-intrusive and efficient way to learn to read *kanji* ideograms. By enabling you to decipher every word immediately, *furigana* helps you grasp the meaning of whole passages faster without needing to get bogged down in fruitless and demoralizing searches for the pronunciation of individual words.

By providing you with the pronunciation, *furigana* also enables you to commit new words to memory right away (since we remember more by sound than by appearance), as well as giving you the wherewithal to look them up, should you want to go beyond the single usage example on the facing English page. *Read Real NIHONGO* provides a mini-glossary on each right page to help you identify and commit to memory the most important words and phrases.

Raw Materials for Conversation

So much for *furigana* and the language-learning aspect—now for the content. The books in this series are all about Japan, from its customs, traditions and cuisine to its history, politics and economy. Providing essential insights into what makes the Japanese and their society tick, every book can help you as you transition from ignorant outsider to informed insider. The information the books contain gives you a treasure trove of raw materials you can use in conversations with Japanese people. Whether you want to amaze your interlocutors with your knowledge of Japanese religion, impress your work colleagues with your mastery of party-seating etiquette and correct bowing angles, or enjoy a heated discussion of the relative merits of arranged marriages versus love marriages, *Read Real NIHONGO* is very much the gift that keeps on giving.

We are confident that this series will help everyone—from students to businesspeople and diplomats to tourists—start reading Japanese painlessly while also learning about Japanese culture. Enjoy!

Tom Christian
Editor-in-Chief
Read Real NIHONGO Series

はじめに

　この2年間、われわれは1つの大きな問題に捕らえられ、振り回されてきた。この問題は、いまだ世界中の人々が対応に苦慮している。われわれの日常、他人との関係、はては国際情勢にまで影響を与えた。この問題のせいで、今まで普通だと思っていた世の中に戻ることはないだろう。個人として、また社会として、失ったものを嘆く人々がいても仕方がない。

　しかし、このパンデミックは、同時にわれわれがそれまであまり注意を払ってこなかった物事について、まるで「ポーズボタン」を押したかのように、一度立ち止まって見直す機会を与えてくれた、と私は思っている。社会、政治、経済など、以前は忙しくて気にとめてこなかった事柄について、われわれは考える機会を与えられた。どうせなら、この厳しい状況を最大限に活用して、自らが置かれた現状を把握し、生活や仕事、互いに対する態度などを改善する新しい具体的な方法を考えてみてはどうだろうか。全ての人にとって住みやすい未来の世界を構築するために、皆が将来を見据えて協力する絶好の機会なのではないかと思う。

　本書の日英対訳方式は、読者が、分からない日本語をいちいち調べなくても読むことができるよう構成されている。日本語訳はパラグラフごとに基本的内容を伝えるようになっているが、必ずしも一語一句が直訳されているわけではないことに留意いただきたい。本書の目的は、それぞれの題材を議論するにあたり、読者が必要とする語彙や表現を学びやすくするためのものであり、翻訳の例文として使用することを目的としているわけではない。

　最後に、読者の皆さんにエールを送りたい——自分が変わる努力をしなければ他人を変えることはできない。皆が恩恵にあずかれるよう、一緒に頑張ろう。

ジェームス・M・バーダマン

2021年12月

Preface

For the past two years, we have been distracted and dismayed by one dominant issue—one that people around the world are still dealing with. It has altered our daily routines, our relationships with others, and international affairs. Because of this issue, we will not return to what was once considered normal. It is understandable if some people choose to lament what has been lost, as individuals and as a society.

But I believe that the pandemic has also provided us with an opportunity, to press "pause" and think seriously about issues we have not paid enough attention to: social, political, and economic issues that in the past we believed we were too busy to deal with. We have time now. We might as well make the best of a tough situation, by first grasping where we are at this point and then working out new concrete ways to improve our way of living, working, and treating each other. It is a chance to envision and to work together to establish a future world that's a better place for everyone.

A brief note: The English-Japanese *taiyaku* format allows the reader to read the Japanese without looking up each unknown word. The Japanese translation conveys the basic message one paragraph at a time, but it is not intended to be a precise word-for-word translation. The purpose of this book is to help the reader learn the helpful English vocabulary and phrases for discussing each topic; it is not intended to serve as a model for translation.

A final word of encouragement: You can't try to change others if you're not working on yourself. Let's all do it, for everyone's benefit.

James M. Vardaman
December 2021

社会 *51*
しゃ　かい
Society

エネルギー・環境 *83*
かんきょう
Energy and Environment

防災 *97*
ぼう さい

Disaster Prevention

教育 *107*
きょう いく

Education

共に生きる *123*
とも い

Living Together

生活・文化　*159*

Daily Life and Culture

政治・経済
せいじ　けいざい

Politics and Economics

01

❏ 新型コロナウイルスの蔓延

日本のコンセンサスはとかく**前例に基づく**ものが多い。そこで大きな問題が発生し、前例がない場合、**組織**は問題解決のために素早く動けないようだ。新型コロナウイルスが徐々に広がってきたとき、国の**堅牢な「縦割り行政」**は**能力不足**のように見えた。前例がなかったので、効果的な対応をとるための省庁間の情報共有や協力体制を築くことができないようだった。

何週間もの間、不安に駆られた日本の人々は、必要となったマスク一つ手に入れることが難しくなった。**当時の安倍首相**は各家庭に2枚のマスクを約束した。各家庭が何人家族であろうと、2枚。この「**アベノマスク**」の話題はメディアを通して世界中に広がった。なぜ、**ジャストインタイム生産方式**や効率的な**物流**、高い生活水準を誇る日本が国民に簡素なマスクを大量に届けることができないのか。多くの国民が、マスク分配システムを素早く開発した若き台湾デジタル担当大臣オードリー・タン氏を見て、日本の政府も日本のオードリーを見つけ出して国ができないことをやってもらえないのだろうかと思った。

感染率の大変高いウイルスの蔓延は新たな深刻な問題を露呈させた。日本にはこのような究極の緊急事態に対応するための仕組みがない。全てが**その場限り**だ。当時の菅首相の下、政府は国民に対して一体何が起こっているか説明し、常に変化する状況に対応する有効な**方策**を講じる意志を示さずにきた。

いわゆる「**自粛**」だけでは状況を改善するのに不十分であることが早い時点で明らかになった。政治家の中には、**緊急事態を宣言できるよう憲法を改正**すべきだと主張する者もいた。それに対する抵抗もあり、いずれにしてもそのような重大な変更のコンセンサスを得るには長い時間がかかる。しかし、なぜ

The COVID-19 Pandemic

Japanese consensus tends to be based on precedent. If a major problem occurs and there is no precedent, then organizations seem unable to react quickly to solve the problem. When the COVID-19 epidemic first began, the air-tight "silos" of government ministries appeared incapable. They did not have precedent to fall back on and they did not seem capable of sharing information and working across bureaucracies to reach an effective response.

For weeks, anxious Japanese struggled to obtain even a single protective mask, when it was clear that everyone needed them. Then Prime Minister Abe promised that each family would receive two masks. Two masks, regardless of how many people were in each family. The "Abenomask" meme spread across media worldwide. How could Japan, which was once admired for its just-in-time production methods, efficient delivery system, and high standard of living, not be able to im-mediately deliver large supplies of simple masks to its citizens? Many citizens looked at Audrey Tang, Taiwan's young Digital Minister who quickly organized a system for mask distribution, and wondered why the Japanese government didn't try to find another Audrey to do what the government could not do.

The spread of the highly contagious virus showed another serious problem. Japan does not have a system for dealing with such extreme emergencies. Everything seems makeshift. The national government, under then Prime Minister Suga, exhibited little initiative in trying to clarify what was happening and establish effective policies for dealing with the constantly changing situation.

It quickly became clear that calling for "voluntary self-re-straint," *jishuku*, was far from adequate. Political figures began calling for a change in the Constitution to allow for declaration of a state of emergency. But there was resistance to that, and anyway, reaching a consensus on such a critical change would take a very long time. But why would the government not pass an emergency measure, with a time limit, that would allow it to

□前例に基づく based on precedent

□組織 organization

□堅牢な robust

□縦割り行政 vertically segmented administrative system

□能力不足 incapable

□省庁間の interagency

□当時の then

□首相 Prime Minister

□アベノマスク *Abenomask* is a colloquial term for gauze cloth masks that were distributed in Japan from April 2020 amid the COVID-19 pandemic.

□ジャストインタイム生産方式 just-in-time production methods

□物流 delivery system

□感染率の大変高い highly contagious

□露呈させた exposed

□その場限り makeshift

□方策 measure

□自粛 voluntary self-restraint

□緊急事態宣言 declaration of a state of emergency

□憲法 Constitution

政府は特定の活動を制限する緊急事態宣言を可能にする**時限付きの緊急措置を法制化**しないのだろうか。誰かが最初の一歩を踏み出すのを待つのではなく、政府の中の誰かがイニシアチブを取るべきだ。しかし、そこまでの想像力を持つ者はいなかった。

代わりに政府と**都道府県知事**は、誰が何をすべきかについてやり取りをし続けた。誰一人として変化する**危機的状況**をなんとかコントロールするために罰則を伴うロックダウンを宣言するつもりはないようだった。代わりに、短期の規制をもって職場や学校、個人の集会に時間や規模の制限を設けた。例えば、午後7時までしか店で酒を提供することができない、などだ。これなど全く意味不明だ。

レストランや居酒屋は大きな打撃を受けた。もしも国民の大多数が**ワクチン接種**を受けるまでの間、完全なシャットダウンを**維持**できていれば、**安全を担保**しつつ徐々にこういった商売は再開することができただろう。代わりに、**感染者数**が下がるまで短期的な時間制限を設けるという**手段が講じられた**。そして再開すると、再び**感染率**が上がる。こうした開けては閉めての繰り返しが国民の**不評を買った**。ワクチンの供給や接種方法に関する**情報の周知**の遅れが、さらに国民の不満を募らせた。

政府内のあらゆるレベルの人間や日本の国民がこのような経験から何も学ばなかったのであれば、残念なことだ。緊急事態宣言を出すことに対しては深い議論と**迅速な決断**が必要である。誰ができるのか。どのように実施するのか。規制に反する人々をどうするのか。日本人は「自粛」は得意かもしれないが、パンデミックのような**事変**には、それでは不十分だ。次の選挙の心配をするより、全ての政党の政治家は、このような**極限状態**での無能力さの露呈を繰り返させないよう、専門家から情報を集めて互いにルール作りに協力し合うべきである。

政治・経済

Politics and Economics

declare a state of emergency with specific levels of prohibited activities? Rather than looking around for someone to make a first move, someone in the government should have taken initiative. But no one had enough imagination to do that.

Instead, the Prime Minister's Cabinet and the country's prefectural governors went back and forth regarding who should do what. No one seemed ready to completely declare a lockdown—with penalties for infringement—in order to gain some control over the evolving crises. Instead, short-term restrictions were put into place, setting time limits and capacity limits for businesses, schools, and private gatherings. It was okay to drink alcohol in a restaurant until 7:00 p.m. but not after that. This made no sense at all.

The restaurant and *izakaya* trade suffered enormously. If there had been a sustained, complete shutdown until large portions of the population were vaccinated, then there could have been a gradual, continuous reopening of these businesses with safety for everyone. Instead, there were short-term, time-limited periods leading to lower figures of infections. Then as things reopened, the infection rates rose again. This start-stop-start cycle repeated itself to the dismay of the public. Delays in vaccine distribution and in publicizing the times and places where vaccination was available left the public even more disgruntled.

It would be unfortunate if the various levels of government and the people themselves fail to learn from these experiences. There needs to be a deep discussion and a rapid decision regarding the declaring of a state of emergency. Who can do it? How should it be enforced? What do you do with people who break restrictions? Japanese may be good at "voluntary self-restraint," but that is insufficient in events like the pandemic. Instead of worrying about the next election, politicians of all parties ought to collaborate in getting new expert information and laying down rules so that there is no repeat of this incompetence in dealing with extreme conditions.

□時限付きの　with a time limit
□緊急措置　emergency measure
□法制化する　legislate
□都道府県知事　prefectural governor
□危機的状況　critical situation
□全く意味不明だ　make no sense at all
□ワクチン接種を受ける　vaccinated
□維持する　sustain
□安全を担保する　ensuring safety
□感染者　infected person
□手段を講じる　take measures
□感染率　infection rate
□不評を買う　receive unfavorable criticism
□情報の周知　publicizing information
□迅速な　rapid
□事変　crisis, disaster
□極限状態　extreme condition

02

❏ **東京 2020**（2021）**オリンピック**

政治・経済

Politics and Economics

　一部の人々の間で、2020オリンピックは「**復興五輪**」と呼ばれていた。これは、巨大地震、大津波と**福島第一原発**のメルトダウンを伴った2011年の大災害からの復興を意味する。大震災のもたらした被害、**強制退去**、トラウマは**前代未聞**のものであった。

　だがオリンピックを使って、世界に日本が大規模な災害から立ち直ったことを示すのはかなり**的外れ**だ。オリンピックは国同士の友好を育み、世界のトップアスリートを**讃える**場である。ホスト国が政治利用するためのツールではない。被災地の住民の中には、復興五輪と呼ぶことで日常生活を破壊されたことから立ち直ろうとする**地元民**の強さを示す機会と捉えた者がいたかもしれない。また中には、まだ復興の**過程**にある状況に対して、もっと努力と政府の援助が必要だと主張するための表現の一つとして使う者もいたかもしれない。**いずれにしても**、この表現を希望と決意を表すものとして使った地元民を非難することは難しいだろう。

　一方、国のレベルでこの表現を使った人は、誰も福島第一原発の今の現実を理解していないように思う。あそこには完全な「復興」はなく、この先何十年も「復興」はない。国のリーダーが繰り返しオリンピックを**形容する**のに使った「**安心・安全**」はない。しかし、国のリーダーたちやオリンピック委員会のメンバーのほとんどは「福島」と言うことを避けた。彼らは、**敷地内で汚染水**を入れたタンクが増え続け、ほぼ**手付かず**のまま放置されている大量の**放射性デブリ**について述べることを避けるのに必死だったようだ。

The 2020 (2021) Olympics

In some circles, the 2020 Olympics were called something else: *Fukko Gorin* (the Recovery Olympics). The reference, of course, was to recovery from the 2011 disaster, which combined a tremendous earthquake, enormous tsunami, and nuclear meltdowns at the Fukushima No. 1 nuclear power plant. The damage, displacement, and trauma were unprecedented.

Taking the Olympics as an occasion to show the world that Japan had recovered from the widespread damage seemed considerably off-key. The Olympics are supposed to build friendship between nations and provide an occasion to celebrate the best athletes in the world. They are not designed to serve as a political tool within the host country. Some residents of the local disaster area referred to the Recovery Olympics as an occasion for showing the toughness of the local people, who had made every effort to overcome the destruction of their daily lives. Some perhaps used the expression to draw renewed attention to the fact that more effort and more government support were necessary in the ongoing process. Whichever the case, it is hard to criticize local people for using the expression to represent hope and determination.

However, anyone at the national level who used the expression clearly did not have a grasp of the current reality at the Fukushima No. 1 nuclear power station. There is no full "recovery" there and there will not be a "recovery" for decades to come. It is not "safe and secure," as Japan's leaders constantly referred to the Olympics themselves. But most of the national leaders and Japan Olympic Committee members did their best not to mention the word "Fukushima." They seemed anxious to avoid mentioning the fact that nuclear contaminated water was being kept in an expanding number of tanks around the facility and huge amount of nuclear debris remained virtually untouched.

□復興　recovery
□五輪　Olympics
□津波　tsunami
□福島第一原発　Fukushima No. 1 nuclear power plant
□大震災　great earthquake (disaster)
□強制退去　displacement
□前代未聞　unprecedented
□的外れ　off-key
□讃える　celebrate
□地元民　local people
□〜の過程にある　in the process of
□いずれにしても　whichever the case
□形容する　describe
□敷地　site
□（放射能）汚染水　nuclear contaminated water
□手付かずの　untouched
□放射性デブリ　nuclear debris

　全てが「前例」に従っていれば、日本は2022年までオリンピックを延期しても正当な判断と見なされただろう。それまでには多くのステークホルダーもワクチン接種が終わり、世界中から観戦者を受け入れることができただろう。しかし、日本人や他国の大多数の人々にワクチン接種を受けさせる明確で現実的な計画もないまま2021年までしか延期をしなかったことで、日本をおとぎ話の国に仕立ててしまったのだ。誰も不測の事態を想定せずともよい理想的な状況。なんとかなるさ。「想定外」な問題が存在しないところ。想像できないのであれば、選択肢を考える必要はない。

　日本はいいかげんに仮定の問題や可能性にも対応するようにならなければいけない。日本は歴史的に変化に対応してきた。今もそうしなければならない。

If all had gone according to "precedent," Japan might have been justified in carrying on with the Olympics with a delay until 2022. By then, perhaps the various stakeholders could have gotten everyone vaccinated and preparations could have been made to accept spectators from around the world. But delaying until only 2021 without a clear and realistic plan for vaccinating the Japanese and the majority of people in other nations left Japan in never-never land. This is a utopian situation, where one doesn't have to consider any contingencies. Things will work out, somehow. This is where *soteigai*, potential issues, do not exist. If it can't be imagined, then there is no need to consider options for responding.

Japan needs to start dealing with hypothetical questions, potential cases. Japan has adapted to changes before in its history, and it must do so again.

□前例　precedent
□観戦者　spectator
□おとぎ話の国　never-never land
□仕立てる　turn ~ into
□不測の事態　contingency
□想定外な問題　potential issues
□選択肢　option
□いいかげんに　properly
□仮定の　hypothetical

03

❏ 日本政府のデジタル化

政治・経済

Politics and Economics

日本は世界でも最高水準のモバイルやブロードバンドネットワークを所有する国ではあるが、政府機関は紙の書類やハンコを使った承認からいまだに逃れられずにいる。**行政改革担当大臣**だった河野太郎氏は就任時、**行政手続き**において個人の**認印**を必要とするものが推定1万5000件にのぼると述べた。その後、件数は大幅に減少した。

2021年初め『エコノミスト』誌に掲載された「アップデートが必要」とお茶目に題された記事によると、OECD内の30カ国で行われた調査の結果、デジタル技術を活用した行政サービスの割合は日本が**最下位**であった。2018年、同調査のトップを走るアイスランドでは、国民は行政手続きの80%をオンラインで**申請**できるそうだ。日本では、同様の手続きをオンラインで行っている国民はたったの7.3%のみだ。日本は**古びた**ファクスやめったにアップデートされないウェブサイト、申請のために自ら役所に足を運ぶことに**ご執心**のようだ。

国や行政が**執行する**行政手続きは**推定**で5万6000種類もあるとされる。しかし、2019年時点で、オンラインのみにて完結するものはたったの7.5%だ。新設される**デジタル庁**はやることがたくさんありそうだ。メディアや一般人の多くは、台湾で人気のデジタル担当大臣オードリー・タン氏の日本人版が必要ではないかと主張する。

コロナ禍で、政府も国民もデジタル化が**急務**であることを認識した。国によってはたった数週間で家庭や企業に**現金を給付**できているが、日本では何ヵ月もかかり、しばしば複数の手書きの書類を提出するために役所に通わなければいけなかった。

Digitizing Japanese Government

While Japan has some of the world's best mobile and broadband networks, its government agencies seem unable to escape from paper documents and authorizing services with a *hanko*. Then minister for administrative reform, Taro Kono, estimated at the beginning of his time in that position that in some 15,000 cases, a personal seal was required to carry out a bureaucratic procedure. That has since been significantly reduced.

According to an article in *The Economist* in early 2021 entertainingly titled "Update required," in a survey of 30 countries in the OECD, Japan came in last place in terms of the percentage of the digital services that the government provides. In 2018, in Iceland, the top runner, 80% of its citizens requested something from the government online. In Japan, only 7.3% of its citizens used online services for that purpose. Japan seems attached to antiquated fax machines, rarely updated websites, and personal visits to offices to carry out applications.

It is estimated that there are some 56,000 administrative procedures that are carried out by the national government. As of 2019, however, only 7.5% could be completed online. It would seem that the new ministry of digital reform has a lot of work to do. Members of the media and the public at large have suggested that Japan needs its own version of Taiwan's popular digital minister, Audrey Tang.

The pandemic made the need for rapid digitization clear to the government and the public as well. While some nations managed to send out cash relief to families and businesses within weeks, Japan's payments took months and often required multiple visits to government offices to submit multiple handwritten forms just to apply for payments.

□ 水準　level

□ 承認　authorizing

□ 逃れられず　unable to escape

□ 行政改革担当大臣　minister for administrative reform

□ 行政手続き　bureaucratic procedure

□ 認印　unofficial and unregistered personal seal

□ お茶目に　mischievously

□ 最下位　come in the last place

□ 申請する　apply for

□ 古びた　antiquated

□ ～にご執心のようだ　seem attached to

□ 執行する　carry out

□ 推定では　It is estimated that

□ デジタル庁　Digital Agency

□ 禍　disaster

□ 急務である　It is a pressing need

□ 現金を給付する　provide cash

　これを変えるのは容易ではない。国の機関では、各省庁が独自に「デジタル構築」している。さらに地方自治体レベルでもそれぞれ独自のシステムを所有している。これらの組織がデータ共有できるように、互換性のあるシステムを開発するには時間がかかる。また、このようなオンラインの手続きが不得手な高齢者からの反発もあるだろう。

　地方自治体の窓口に勤める地方公務員が、行政サービスを受けるためのデジタル機器を持ち合わせない高齢者に対応するITサポート要員になる必要が生じるかもしれない。コロナワクチン接種の予約では、それが必要不可欠だということが明らかになった。ITが得意でデジタル機器を所有している住民ですら、接種の予約を取るのは至難の業であった。機器も知識もない高齢者は、今までと同じ行動を取った。役所に行って手伝ってもらうしかなかったのだ。

　IT化の恩恵は明らかである。時間や紙の消費の無駄を削減し、9時5時で働く人が時間外でも書類を入手することができ、生産性も上がる。しかし、そのためには日本政府のもののやり方を大幅に変えていかなければならない。

Changing this will not be easy. At the national level, each ministry and agency has its own "digital architecture." Below this, each local government has its own version. It will take time for these entities to develop compatible systems that make sharing data possible. There will also be resistance from the elderly, who will not have the skills required for carrying out procedures online.

It may require that the local bureaucrats at local government office counters become digital-assistance workers helping older residents and citizens without their own digital devices apply for services. That this is essential was made clear during the vaccination registration process. Finding vaccination sites with available slots was hard enough for digitally savvy residents with devices at home. Older residents with neither the devices nor the skills had to do what they had always done: go to the municipal office and ask for assistance.

The benefits of digitization are clear. It saves time, reduces the consumption of paper, allows people to apply for or receive documents outside of regular 9-to-5 work hours, and increases productivity. But it will require a considerable adjustment in how Japan's government operates.

□デジタル構築している
　digitalizing its services
□互換性のある　compatible
□反発　resistance
□地方自治体　local
　government office
□地方公務員　local
　government employee
□必要不可欠　essential
□〜するのは至難の業　It is
　very difficult to
□恩恵　benefit
□消費　consumption

❏ 皇位継承（こういけいしょう）

政治・経済（せいじ・けいざい）

Politics and Economics

徳仁親王（なるひとしんのう）が天皇（てんのう）に即位（そくい）し、新（あら）たに令和（れいわ）の時代（じだい）が始（はじ）まった今（いま）、将来女性天皇（しょうらいじょせいてんのう）を容認（ようにん）するかどうかの議論（ぎろん）は急務（きゅうむ）ではなくなったように思（おも）われる。しかし、皇位継承者（こういけいしょうしゃ）は3人（にん）しかいない。天皇（てんのう）の弟（おとうと）である秋篠宮親王（あきしののみやしんのう）、天皇（てんのう）の甥（おい）である悠仁親王（ひさひとしんのう）、それに天皇（てんのう）の叔父（おじ）に当（あ）たる常陸宮親王（ひたちのみやしんのう）である。皇位継承者（こういけいしょうしゃ）が3人（にん）しかおらず、そのうちお1人（ひとり）が高齢（こうれい）となると、1947年（ねん）に制定（せいてい）された皇室典範（こうしつてんぱん）の改正（かいせい）が必要（ひつよう）なのではないかという議論（ぎろん）も上（あ）がってくる。

現在（げんざい）の皇室典範（こうしつてんぱん）は、皇位継承者（こういけいしょうしゃ）が男性（だんせい）であることを定（さだ）めている。制限（せいげん）はそれだけではない。さらに皇位継承者（こういけいしょうしゃ）は父方（ちちかた）（父系（ふけい）の男性皇族（だんせいこうぞく））から選（えら）ばれなければならないと定（さだ）められている。同典範（どうてんぱん）では、徳仁天皇（なるひとてんのう）と雅子皇后（まさここうごう）の唯一（ゆいいつ）の子（こ）である愛子内親王（あいこないしんのう）は皇位継承者（こういけいしょうしゃ）に当（あ）てはまらない。女性（じょせい）であるからだ。

政府（せいふ）はあらゆる分野（ぶんや）の専門家（せんもんか）を集（あつ）めて有識者会議（ゆうしきしゃかいぎ）を開催（かいさい）している。専門家（せんもんか）の中（なか）には父系（ふけい）の女性（じょせい）による皇位継承（こういけいしょう）を歓迎（かんげい）する者（もの）もいるが、母系（ぼけい）の皇位継承（こういけいしょう）を認（みと）める者（もの）は少（すく）ない。しかし、いずれの専門家（せんもんか）も、何（なん）らかの方法（ほうほう）で現在（げんざい）の3人（にん）から皇位継承者（こういけいしょうしゃ）の数（かず）を増（ふ）やすことが重要（じゅうよう）であると考（かんが）えている。

Imperial Succession

With the succession of former Prince Naruhito to the imperial throne and the beginning of the Reiwa era, the issue of whether a female monarch would be allowed to ascend the throne in the future seemed less urgent. However, there are only three heirs in line to succeed Emperor Naruhito. They are his younger brother, Crown Prince Akishino, his nephew Prince Hisahito, and his uncle, Prince Hitachi. With only three in the current order of imperial succession—one of whom is already of advanced age—there is concern that changes to the 1947 Imperial House Law are needed.

The present law limits heirs to the throne to males. That is one limitation. The law also states that the heir has to have an emperor on his father's side. The law obviously eliminates Emperor Naruhito and Empress Masako's only child, Princess Aiko, because she is female.

The government appointed an advisory panel which has heard from experts from various fields. Some experts welcome succession by women in patrilineal imperial succession. Few welcome succession through a maternal line. But most of the experts who have presented opinions seem to feel it is important to consider some way of expanding the number in the line of succession beyond the current three princes.

□親王　imperial prince

□皇位継承者　heir to the throne

□甥　nephew

□叔父　uncle

□皇室典範　Imperial House Law

□父方　on one's father's side

□内親王　imperial princess

□有識者会議　advisory panel

□父系の　patrilineal

□母系の　maternal

05

❑ 政治スキャンダル——赤木ファイル

政治・経済
Politics and Economics

　ここ数年の報道において、とかく目にするようになった曖昧な単語がある。それは「忖度」だ。この言葉の意味は、会社や役所などで、部下が上司に取り入るために先んじて行動することである。簡単に言うと、上司が認める、または安心することを知っているがゆえに、言われなくても何かをすることだ。ここで重要なのは、上司が直接命令するわけではないということだ。部下は上司の無言の意向を「読んで」行動に移す。

　2017年、財務省による当時の安倍晋三首相と森友学園にまつわる書類改ざんは、忖度とは逆のスキャンダルとなった。ここでは総理大臣夫人と関係のある学校の広大な政府所有地に関する売買について直接命令が下された。その証拠がいわゆる「赤木ファイル」の存在だ。当時、大阪府の職員であった赤木俊夫氏が518ページにも及ぶ書類を作成したが、自らの行為を苦にして自殺した。ファイル自体は2021年に赤木氏の妻に渡った。この書類には、誰が土地売買の記録改ざんを指示し、公文書改ざんという不法行為をもたらしたか記されている。

　このファイルで赤木氏は、すでに承認された記録を改ざんしたり書き直したりしてはいけない、と書き残している。赤木氏の妻に渡された書類では、赤木氏に改ざんを命じた上司の名前が黒塗りされていた。書類の改ざんを命じた張本人は財務省の佐川宣寿理財局長だと言われていた。佐川氏が当時の総理大臣とその夫人に「忖度」したのではないかとの疑念が残った。

Political Scandals: The "Akagi File" Scandal

A rather obscure term has appeared regularly in the media in recent years: *sontaku*. This Japanese word describes subordinates in business or in government offices preemptively acting to ingratiate themselves with their superiors. In simple terms, they do something without being told to do it, because they know their superiors will be pleased or relieved. It is a means of gaining favor with the bosses. The key element is that the boss never actually gives a direct order to do something. The subordinate "reads" the unspoken desire of the superior and acts on it.

High-profile document-tampering involving the Finance Ministry, then-Prime Minister Abe, and Moritomo Gakuen in 2017 became a scandal that was the reverse of *sontaku*. In this scandal concerning the sale of a state-owned plot of land at an enormous discount to a school linked to the wife of Prime Minister Abe, the order was direct. Evidence for this was found in the so-called "Akagi file." The 518-page document collection was compiled by Toshio Akagi, a ministry official in Osaka Prefecture, who committed suicide due to stress that resulted from his activities. The file itself became available to Akagi's wife in 2021. It includes documents on who gave instructions to alter records of the land sale, resulting in illegal tampering of government documents.

Akagi wrote in these documents that already-approved records should not be revised or reworded. He also wrote that he was instructed to doctor the files by a superior whose name was blacked out in the copy delivered to Akagi's widow. Nobuhisa Sagawa, director-general of the ministry's Financial Bureau, was suspected of being the ultimate source of the instructions to alter the documents. Skepticism remained as to whether Sagawa was practicing *sontaku* in an attempt to protect the Prime Minister and his wife.

□曖昧な obscure

□忖度 act of guessing and following what someone else wants or expects, without being told directly

□取り入る ingratiate

□先んじて preemptively

□意向 intention

□財務省 Ministry of Finance

□書類改ざん document-tampering

□公文書 government document

□黒塗り blacked out

□張本人 mastermind

□理財局長 director-general of the Financial Bureau

□疑念 suspicion

06

□ 献身的に働きすぎる日本人

政治・経済

Politics and Economics

　日本における戦後の経済復興は、シビアな交換条件の上に実現したものだ。企業は従業員を生涯にわたって面倒を見る代わりに、従業員がキャリアの全てを企業に捧げることを求める。企業にとって全ての従業員を不景気な時も含めて雇い続けることにはリスクもあるが、手法としては基本的に成功している。

　しかし、従業員は一連の犠牲を強いられる。残業続きで家庭での時間を犠牲にする。単身赴任によって伴侶や子供との関係を犠牲にする。その結果の一つに「過労死」が挙げられる。今や英語の辞書にも載っている言葉だ。例えば、要求の高さで悪名高い公共放送のNHKで働く31歳の記者は心臓疾患で亡くなった。後に、彼女は死ぬ1ヵ月前に159時間も残業し、休日はたった2日しかなかったことが判明した。

　これに対する問題意識は次第に高まっている。多くの場合、職場で「調和」や「協力」を重視するあまりに生じた悪しき結果である。従業員は上司や同僚が帰る前に退社することを躊躇する。先に帰ることは、失礼で思いやりのない、不誠実なことと考える。

　それに対して、このように「よく働く人」が実際成果を上げているのだろうかという問題もある。生産性や効率を上げれば、通常の勤務時間を超えて残る必要はない、と主張する者もいる。年功序列ではなく実績で給料を決めることがこの問題を解決する一つの手立てではないだろうか。

Dedication to Overworking

Japan brought about its postwar economic boom through a tough bargain. Companies agreed to look after their employees for life in exchange for a willingness to dedicate their entire careers to the company. For the companies, it was risky to keep everyone on the payrolls, even during a business downturn, but it was basically successful as a strategy.

For the employees, however, it was a series of sacrifices. Sacrifice home life for late hours at the office, working overtime. Sacrifice relations with spouse and children, by being transferred to another city, while the other members of the family stay in the original home. The possible result has been expressed in the word *karoshi*, death by overwork, now found in English dictionaries. As one example, a 31-year-old reporter for the notoriously demanding public broadcaster NHK died of heart failure. Authorities later determined that she had regularly worked as much as 159 hours of overtime per month and had had only two days off in the month prior to her death.

There is an increase in awareness of the problem. In many cases, it is a malignant result of emphasis on "harmony" and "cooperation" in the workplace. Employees hesitate to leave the office before their bosses, and even before their peers. Leaving first, they think, would be rude, inconsiderate, or disloyal.

In contrast to this is the issue of whether these "hard workers" are actually accomplishing much. If they increased their productivity and efficiency, some claim, there would be no reason to stay beyond the regular working hours. Paying workers for performance rather than seniority would be a start in solving this problem.

- □ 戦後　postwar
- □ 経済復興　economic reconstruction
- □ シビアな　severe
- □ 交換条件　exchange conditions
- □ 生涯にわたって　over the course of one's life
- □ 面倒を見る　look after
- □ 捧げる　dedicate
- □ 不景気な時　during a business downturn
- □ 手法　method
- □ 一連の　a series of
- □ 犠牲　sacrifice
- □ 単身赴任　working separated from one's family
- □ 伴侶　spouse
- □ 過労死　death by overwork
- □ 公共放送　public broadcaster
- □ 心臓疾患　heart failure
- □ 調和　harmony
- □ 悪しき結果　malignant result
- □ 躊躇する　hesitate
- □ 思いやりのない　inconsiderate
- □ 不誠実　disloyal
- □ それに対して　In contrast to this
- □ 年功序列　promotion by seniority

しかし、多くの企業は改革に対して消極的である。むしろ、従業員は記録に残さず残業代が支払われない「**サービス残業**」を強いられる。従業員がこのやり方を拒絶するのは難しい。彼らは、**忠誠心、献身、やる気**を示したいのである。しかし、**悲惨な結果**になることもある。1つの有名な例に、**広告代理店電通**の社員が長時間労働のプレッシャーから自殺したケースがある。彼女は数ヵ月にわたり、月100時間以上も残業していたのだ。

国は残業の**上限**を月100時間とする法律を制定した。しかし、こう考えてみてはどうか。100時間とは、週50時間労働が2週に及ぶことだ。つまり、6週間分の仕事を4週間に**詰め込む**ことになる。たまに1週間のうち数時間の残業を課すことはありうるかもしれないが、週25時間の残業が**常態化する**のはおかしいだろう。

このところ、企業は正社員を増やすことを拒んできた。代わりに、正社員としての採用の道も**確約されない契約社員**を使ってきた。彼らは正社員と同じ仕事を半分の給料でやらされ、法律上、正社員として雇用されなければならなくなる直前に契約解除となる。

Yet many companies have seemed unmoved by calls for reform. To the contrary, they have their employees do "service" overtime, that is, working overtime without logging it or receiving extra pay. This pattern is hard for employees to refuse. They want to show loyalty, dedication, and determination. But the results can be disastrous. As one prominent example, in 2015 an employee of the advertising company Dentsu committed suicide due to pressure from excessive working hours. She had worked over 100 hours of overtime for several months in a row.

The Diet has passed a law that limits overtime to a maximum of 100 hours per month. But think about it this way: 100 hours is roughly two 50-hour workweeks. That means squeezing six weeks of work into a four-week month. It may be reasonable to ask employees to work a few hours extra during one week on occasion, but not 25 extra hours a week on a regular basis.

All the while, companies have refused to hire additional full-time employees. Instead, they have used a system that allows contracted employees, who they can hire with no promise of a later shift to full-time status. These workers do the job of regular employees, at usually less than half of the salary, and are released just prior to the date when they would have to be given full-time status under the law.

□サービス残業　working overtime without pay

□忠誠心　loyalty

□献身　dedication

□やる気　determination

□悲惨な　disastrous

□広告代理店　advertising company

□電通　Dentsu Inc.

□上限　upper limit

□詰め込む　cram

□常態化する　normalize

□確約されない　not guaranteed

□契約社員　contract employee

07

❏ TQCは何処へ

政治・経済

Politics and Economics

　一時、日本は品質管理の賞であるデミング賞の候補と目され、**統合的品質管理（TQC）**を目指すという素晴らしい 志 を持っていたように思う。全ての分野において高い品質を追求する姿勢は世界から称賛された。

　しかし、すでに2017年には日本株式会社の腕は鈍り始めたようで、その目標を達成する気はないと言われ始めた。**合成繊維や樹脂の大手化学企業**である東レは、同年に**子会社**が自動車用タイヤで使われる**タイヤコード**の製品データを改ざんしていたと発表した。三菱マテリアルは、航空機や車に使うアルミの**データ不正**を公表した。日産は、技術者が**有資格者**の検査員のハンコを借りて車体の機能確認を行ったと公表。こうした行為は40年もの間続いていたという。

　さらに2021年、トヨタは都内の販売店で565台のレクサス車に車検を行う際、**法的基準**を満たす値に**改ざんする**など**不正**を行ったと公表した。

　今や品質管理が日本のビジネスにおける**武器**ではない、とまでは誰も言わないが、繰り返される謝罪が**示唆する**のは、日本に求められるスタンダードを全ての人が満たしているわけではないということだ。**内部告発者**などいなくても、状況を改善することはできるだろう。

Where did TQC go?

Japan as a country once seemed to be a candidate for the Deming Prize, an award for quality control, and seemed to aim for total quality control (TQC), an impressive aspiration. The world admired its devotion to high quality in every field.

But as early as 2017, it became apparent that corporate Japan was losing its polish and it began to admit that it wasn't always achieving that goal. Textiles and chemical giant Toray Industries in that year admitted that a subsidiary had faked inspection on cords used in car tires. Mitsubishi Materials confessed that it had been falsifying data on aluminum used in aircraft and cars. Nissan admitted that technicians had borrowed *hanko* from qualified inspectors to approve vehicle checks instead of having the inspectors do the job. The latter misconduct had gone on for 40 years.

In 2021 Toyota confessed that after-sale safety inspection data affecting 565 luxury Lexus cars were manipulated so that they would meet legal standards at a dealership in Tokyo.

No one believes that quality control is no longer part of Japan's business arsenal, but as the repeated acts of apology indicate, not everyone is reaching the standards that one expects from Japan. It shouldn't take whistle-blowers or insider leaks to make things work better.

□デミング賞　Deming Prize
□統合的品質管理　total quality control
□志　aspiration
□合成繊維　synthetic fiber
□樹脂　resin
□化学企業　chemical company
□子会社　subsidiary
□タイヤコード　tire cord
□データ不正　falsifying data
□有資格者　qualified person
□法的基準　legal standard
□改ざんする　falsify
□不正　fraud
□武器　arsenal
□示唆する　indicate
□内部告発者　whistle-blower

08

❏ 企業や政治家の謝罪

政治・経済

Politics and Economics

　日本のテレビに慣れた外国人にとって、ニュース番組のわかりやすい特徴の一つが、公式に謝罪する者たちの見せしめだ。企業や役所のトップ1〜3人がテーブルの後ろに並び、頭を深く下げて謝罪する間、集まった新聞社のカメラマンたちがその人物たちの後頭部の写真を撮る。彼らが何秒間頭を下げたままでいるかを数えるのが一つの余興となっている。

　謝罪会見では何が起こったかを説明するが、具体的に誰が責任を負うのかは明確に言わない。しかし、いつも決まったせりふがある——「このたびは深くお詫びいたします。このようなことが二度と起こらないよう最善を尽くします」。

　官僚も企業人も、それぞれの組織で上り詰める過程で、セミナーなどに参加して謝罪の仕方を学ぶのだろう、と憶測したくなるのは否めない。今回はなんとか許してもらって、この先数ヵ月、数年の間は、このように人前に出る必要がないことを彼らは祈っているのではないだろうか、という印象を視聴者は持つ。しかし、彼らが真摯な態度で改善の約束を積極的に果たすだろうという期待を視聴者が抱くことはない。所詮、言葉は単なる言葉だからだ。

Apologies by Companies and Politicians

To a non-Japanese who is used to Japanese television, one of the obvious features of news programs is the parade of official apologizers. Between one and three top executives of a company or some bureaucracy stand behind a table, make an apology, and bow deeply while assembled newspaper photographers take photos of the top of their heads. One of the entertaining elements is to count how many seconds they will stay bowed before they straighten up.

The apology is a statement of what has occurred, but does not usually mention exactly who was responsible. But there is always a phrase that conveys the message: "We apologize from the depths of our hearts. And we will make sincere efforts to guarantee that this will never happen again."

One would be forgiven for assuming that government and business leaders learn to perform this act of contrition in a seminar as they climb the ladder to the top in their respective hierarchies. It leaves the viewer with a sense that they are hoping to get off the hook this time and won't have to make another appearance in the coming months or years. But it does not give the viewer a sense that they are sincere or that they will actively care out their promises to make improvements. Words are just words.

□見せしめ　example

□後頭部　top of one's head

□余興　entertaining element

□謝罪会見　press conference to apologize

□決まったせりふ　fixed phrase

□最善を尽くす　make sincere efforts

□企業人　corporate person

□上り詰める　climb the ladder to the top

□憶測する　assume

□否めない　can't deny

□真摯な　sincere

国際関係

International Relations

❏ 自衛隊
じえいたい

09

日本は名称を除けば事実上の軍隊を有している。その主眼は防衛である。例えば、潜水艦を見つけ出し、戦闘機を追いやり、日本の国土を飛び越えることができるミサイルの発射を監視する。全ての攻撃任務は、必要となった場合、日本に在留する米軍に任されている。

日本はGDPの１％以下に防衛費を抑えるという自らに課した規制を維持している。現在、最新の攻撃能力を保有する兵器に日本最大の軍艦「いずも」がある。自衛隊はあくまでも「護衛艦」であるとし、その攻撃能力を低く見せている。しかし、甲板上に並ぶF-35戦闘機の列を見れば、それが事実上は空母であることは明白である。さらなる増強計画には、射程距離が長いスタンドオフミサイルの航空機発射型の導入がある。毎年何百回と領空侵犯を繰り返す中国に対して日本の戦闘機がスクランブル発進を繰り返すことを考えれば、これは抑止力になるかもしれない。

直近の課題は、東シナ海の尖閣諸島海域への領海侵犯を繰り返す中国への対応であろう。中国は釣魚島と呼び領有権を主張するが、日本が実効支配している。2021年に入ると中国で新しい海警法が施行され、法律の施行活動の一環と称した領海周辺での中国の動きの活発化に対する懸念が強まっている。この新法では、外国船や個人を領海から撤去させるために、海警局に対して武器の使用を認めている。これは国際法上も日本の海上保安庁法上も認められることではない。もしも中国の海警局が中国の第２の海軍と化しても、日本の海上保安庁は自らの役割を逸脱して軍事行動を取ることはできない。

東シナ海は日本にとって直接的な脅威ではないが、中国が珊瑚礁に人工島を建設し滑走路やレーダーシステム、ミサイル基地を配備することは脅威となる可能性がある。中国の海上防衛の範囲がより広くなり、日本に対する圧力となるかもしれない。

The Self-Defense Forces

Japan has an army in all but name. Its focus is on defense, such a hunting submarines, warding off warplanes, and keeping an eye on missile launches potentially flying over Japan. All offensive duties are left to American troops stationed in Japan, if such duties should be required.

Japan maintains a self-imposed restriction on defense spending that is 1% and less of the national GDP. The most obvious new offensive capabilities include the upgrade of the *Izumo*, Japan's largest warship. The SDF has downplayed this as "an escort ship." But with a deck full of F-35 jets, it would be hard not so see what it really is: an aircraft-carrier. Another upgrade is the acquisition of long-range missiles that can be fired from a warplane. These might serve as a deterrent, given that Japanese warplanes scramble against Chinese incursions several hundreds of times a year.

An immediate issue for Japan is dealing with frequent Chinese incursions into waters around the Senkaku Islands in the East China Sea. China claims them and calls them Diaoyu, but Japan controls them. The concerns grew larger in 2021 with China's new Coast Guard Law, by which China seems to be intruding on territorial waters conducting what it calls law enforcement activities. The new law gives the Coast Guard the right to use weapons when national sovereignty if being infringed on by foreign organizations and individuals at sea. This is not in accord with international law or with Japan's Coast Guard law. If the Chinese Coast Guard develops into China's second navy, there is no way that the Japan's Coast Guard can go beyond its role and take military action.

Although the South China Sea is not a direct threat to Japan, China's building and occupation of airstrips, radar systems, and missile sites on artificial islands constructed on reefs there also pose a potential problem. They make China's naval reach longer, perhaps long enough to put pressure on Japan.

☐ 主眼　focus
☐ 潜水艦　submarine
☐ 戦闘機　warplane
☐ 国土　homeland
☐ 〜を監視する　keep an eye on
☐ 攻撃任務　offensive duties
☐ 〜に在留する　stationed in
☐ 防衛費　defense spending
☐ 自らに課した規制　self-imposed restriction
☐ 攻撃能力　offensive capability
☐ 護衛艦　escort ship
☐ 甲板　deck
☐ 空母　aircraft-carrier
☐ 射程距離　range (of a missile)
☐ スタンドオフミサイル　standoff missile
☐ 領空侵犯　airspace incursion
☐ 抑止力　deterrent
☐ 東シナ海　East China Sea
☐ 尖閣諸島　Senkaku Islands
☐ 釣魚島　Diaoyu
☐ 実効支配する　take effective control
☐ 海警法　Coast Guard Law
☐ 懸念　concern
☐ 海警局　China Coast Guard
☐ 海上保安庁法　Japan Coast Guard Law
☐ 軍事行動　military action
☐ 直接的な　direct
☐ 脅威　threat
☐ 珊瑚礁　coral reef
☐ 配備する　deploy

10

❏ 台湾関係

国際関係

International Relations

中国が主権を主張する台湾は、日本にとって**公に語られない軍事的・政治**的懸案事項である。**従来、日本は台湾の主権に関しては「戦略的に不明瞭」の**立場をとってきたが、近年の中国の政治的・軍事的野心の拡大を見ると、そのような方針を維持するのは難しくなってきている。

しかし、日本にとってもアメリカにとっても、戦略的透明性への方針転換で台湾を擁護する立場を明確にすることは、同様に問題を含んでいる。

中国が台湾の占領を試みた場合、在日米軍は間違いなく巻き込まれるし、日本にも累が及ぶ。両国の国民で台湾に在住する者たちは、直接的に影響を受ける。

現状では、両国とも、この地域のその他の国同様に、自衛能力を引き上げる必要があるだろう。それはそれぞれの国で意味することが異なる。日本の場合、2018年に陸上自衛隊が初めて日本版**海兵隊**とも称される**水陸機動団**を創設した。離島の防衛や**奪還**の際に有益となる**対艦**や**水陸両用作戦**の専門部隊だ。

アメリカのバイデン政権の下、日本は太平洋地域の政策において日米両国がより強固に協力関係を維持できると自信を持っているかもしれないが、台湾に関する中国からの圧力が近い将来に弱まる**兆し**はない。

Dealing with Taiwan

Claimed by China, Taiwan is an unspoken element in Japan's military and political concerns. Until now Japan's position on Taiwan's sovereignty has purposely been left "strategically ambiguous," but with the recent expansion in China's political and military ambitions, such policies are increasingly untenable.

However, for either Japan or the United States to clearly state its commitment to Taiwan, in a shift to strategic clarity, is equally problematic.

In the event that China attempts to seize the island, American forces in Japan would undoubtedly be drawn in, and so would Japan. Citizens from both nations reside in Taiwan and they would be directly affected.

At present it would seem that both nations—as well as other nations in the region—need to build up their self-defense capabilities. That means different things to each nation. For its own part, Japan established its first marine unit of the ground SDF forces in 2018 and practiced anti-ship and amphibious warfare, which, respectively, would be useful for defending and retaking islands.

Under the Biden administration, Japan probably has a stronger sense of confidence that Japan and the US can work together on policies of the western Pacific. However, pressure from China on Taiwan shows no let up for the near future.

□公に語られない　not publicly discussed
□懸案事項　concern
□従来　until now
□主権　sovereignty
□戦略的に不明瞭　strategically ambiguous
□野心　ambition
□〜を擁護する立場　position in defense of
□累が及ぶ　cause trouble
□陸上自衛隊　ground SDF forces
□海兵隊　Marine Corps
□水陸機動団　Amphibious Rapid Deployment Brigade
□奪還　retaking
□対艦　anti-ship
□水陸両用作戦　amphibious operation
□兆し　sign

❑ イージス・アショア

　2017年に北朝鮮が行った実験で、ミサイルが北海道上空を通過し、1,200キロ先の太平洋に落下した。これが初めてではない。衛星を打ち上げるという口実で、過去にも**類似**の実験を4回行っている。しかし、今回のミサイル発射は**不意を突かれた**ため、通常、地震速報を流す防災無線や携帯電話が警報音を発した。

　世間では日本の米軍基地の危険性について頻繁に議論されているが、一般の日本人は軍事**脅威**についてあまり注意を払ってこなかった。平和や国の安全保障を当たり前のものと感じる無関心な態度を「**平和ぼけ**」と呼ぶ。当時の安倍晋三首相は、このミサイル実験を危険で**前例のない**、国の深刻な脅威と呼んだ。しかし数ヵ月すると、このレトリックも消えて日常が戻ってしまった。

　そこで残ったのが、日本に必要な**民間防衛**が備わっているかどうかという疑問だった。国を守るために十分な**ミサイル迎撃システム**を保有しているのか？　日本の平和憲法を**改正**すべきなのか？

　現在日本が保有するミサイル防衛手段には、限定的なエリアの「**地点防空**」が可能なパトリオット**地対空ミサイル**がある。また、**守備範囲**が日本全国に及ぶイージスシステムを搭載するミサイル護衛艦もある。北朝鮮の脅威が増す昨今、イージス防衛システムを陸でも展開すべく、イージス・アショアという陸上で展開されるシステムを導入するべきだという主張が広がっている。しかし、そのシステムは高価で、日本の防衛費の上限は自ら課したGDPの1％となっている。比較して、韓国はその倍、米国はその3倍の金額を防衛費に充てている。

Aegis Ashore

In 2017, North Korea tested a missile that passed over Hokkaido and crashed into the Pacific Ocean roughly 1,200 kilometers to the east of that island. It was not the first time that North Korea had done this. Under the pretense of launching satellites, North Korea had conducted similar tests four times before. But this time the launch was a surprise and it set off alarms over local loudspeakers and mobile phones which usually announced earthquakes.

Despite frequent public debates about the dangers posed by American bases in Japan, in general Japanese people have not paid too much attention to military threats. They refer to this as *heiwaboke*, a nonchalance that takes peace and national security for granted. Then-Prime Minister Shinzo Abe referred to this particular missile launch as reckless, unprecedented, serious and a grave threat to the country. But after several months, the rhetoric disappeared and things returned to normal.

What remained were questions about whether Japan had the civil defense preparations that were necessary. Did it have the anti-missile systems necessary to keep the country safe? And should Japan amend its pacifist constitution?

Currently Japan's missile defense consists of land-based Patriot batteries that provide limited "point defense" of small areas. Its other component is destroyers with Aegis missile-defense systems that cover the entire country. With the growing threat posed by North Korea, however, there are calls for expanding Aegis systems in land-based systems known as Aegis Ashore. But the systems are expensive and Japan's expenditure on military strength is limited to a self-imposed 1% of GDP. By comparison, South Korea spends double that figure and the U.S. spends more than three times that figure.

□ 類似の   similar
□ 不意を突く   catch someone off guard
□ 平和ぼけ   complacency about peace
□ 前例のない   unprecedented
□ 民間防衛   civil defense
□ ミサイル迎撃システム   anti-missile systems
□ 平和憲法   pacifist constitution
□ 改正する   amend
□ 地点防空   point defense
□ 地対空ミサイル   surface-to-air missile
□ 守備範囲   defensive area

　弾道ミサイル防衛(BMD)の配備が予定されていた施設がある山口県と秋田県も、イージス・アショアの配備には反対を表明した。地元住民は将来の北朝鮮の攻撃の的となるかもしれないことを恐れた。防衛省は2021年米国の新型レーダーSPY-7を陸上ではなく戦艦に搭載すると発表した。SPY-7搭載イージス艦２隻が当面、日本列島を弾道ミサイルから守る「目」となるようだ。

The Aegis Ashore proposal also met opposition in Yamaguchi prefecture and Akita prefecture, which were to be sites of the facilities for ballistic missile defense (BMD). Local residents were not eager to have right in their midst what might become prime targets in some future North Korean attack. The Defense Ministry in 2021 announced that instead of installing the U.S. SPY-7 radar system on land, for which it is designed, Japan would install it on ships. The two new ships, it seems, will serve as "eyes" to protect the Japanese archipelago from ballistic missiles.

□弾道ミサイル防衛　ballistic missile defense

□防衛省　Ministry of Defense

□戦艦　battleship

□日本列島　Japanese archipelago

12

❏ 韓国との関係

国際関係

International Relations

日本と韓国はアメリカにとって重要な同盟国だが、両国は友人というより敵同士のような振る舞いをする。2019年、日本は韓国の製造業者にとって半導体やスマートフォンの材料として不可欠な化学物質の輸出規制を厳格化する措置を発動した。韓国ではこれに対抗して、国内での日本製品の不買運動が起こった。

両国が常に対立する問題に、互いの歴史認識の違いがある。20世紀前半、韓国は日本の植民地であった。日本は同国に経済の近代化をもたらしたが、同時に残忍な支配を、特に1937年から1945年の間に行った。

左派系大統領の文在寅は、2018年に「従軍慰安婦」問題に関する2国間の合意を否定した。何千、何万もの韓国人が旧日本軍の慰安婦として性行為を強要され、中には存命している者もいる。従来の合意では、日本政府が謝罪と反省の気持ちを表明し、被害者財団に10億円を拠出するという内容だった。その上で、韓国は外交においてこの問題を持ち出すことをやめ、ソウル市内の日本大使館前の慰安婦像を撤去するというものだった。

同年、韓国の最高裁は、戦時下に強制労働させられた元徴用工が損害賠償を求めた訴訟で、日本企業2社の賠償責任を認める判決を下した。日本政府は、1965年の友好条約で解決済みだと反論した。以来、日本政府は、この問題はすでに解決済みで、日韓請求権協定の反故を正当化することはできないと主張し続けている。

2国間の軋轢は簡単には解消できない。しかし防衛、諜報活動、安全保障にとって、アメリカの同盟国としての両国の関係は重要である。両国が対立している間、北朝鮮と中国は利する一方である。

Relations with South Korea

While Japan and South Korea are important allies of the United States, the two nations act more like adversaries than friends. In 2019 Japan placed export controls on chemicals essential to South Korean producers of semiconductors and smartphones. South Korea responded by boycotting Japanese brands in local stores.

The regular issue has been their respective interpretations of history. In the first half of the twentieth century Korea was a colony of Japan. Although Japan brought economic modernization to the country, it also brought brutal domination, especially during the period between 1937 and 1945.

The left-leaning president Moon Jae-in in 2018 repudiated an agreement between the two nations regarding the matter of "comfort women." Tens of thousands of Koreans, some still alive, were forced to have sex in Japanese army brothels. The earlier settlement had Japan make a formal apology and pay ¥1 billion to the victims. In exchange, Korea agreed to stop using the issue in diplomacy and to remove the statue of a comfort woman outside Japan's embassy in the capital city.

South Korea's Supreme Court in that same year ruled against two Japanese corporations for conscripting laborers during the war. The court ordered the companies to pay compensation to the victims who survived. Japan responded that the matter had been settled by the friendship treaty established between the countries in 1965. The Japanese government has since then continued to contend that the matter was previously resolved and there is no justification for annulling that agreement.

The friction between the two nations has no easy solution. But in terms of defense, intelligence-gathering, and security, the relationship is a key one, especially since they are both allies of the United States. While the two nations confront each other, North Korea and China stand to benefit considerably.

□ 同盟国　ally
□ 敵同士　mutual enemies
□ 半導体　semiconductors
□ 輸出規制　export controls
□ 規制を厳格化する　make regulations stricter
□ 措置　measure
□ 発動する　issue
□ 植民地　colony
□ 残忍な　brutal
□ 支配　domination
□ 従軍慰安婦　comfort women
□ 存命している　still alive
□ 財団　foundation
□ 撤去する　remove
□ 最高裁　Supreme Court
□ 戦時下　during the war
□ 強制労働　forced labor
□ 徴用工　conscripting laborers
□ 損害賠償を求める　claim damages
□ 訴訟　lawsuit
□ 賠償責任を認める　finding liability for damages
□ 判決を下す　enter a judgment
□ 友好条約　friendship treaty
□ 日韓請求権協定　Agreement Between Japan and the Republic of Korea Concerning the Settlement of Problems in Regard to Property and Claims and Economic Cooperation
□ 反故　annulling
□ 正当化する　justify
□ 軋轢　friction
□ 諜報活動　intelligence activity
□ 利する　stand to benefit

社会

しゃかい

Society

❑ 日本の年金受給者

社会 Society

13

高齢化が世界でも最も早く進んでいる国として、日本は大きな問題に直面している。定年に達した人口をどのように支えていくのか。日本の年金制度は、保険料を40年間支払って定年退職する人に対して満額を支給する。しかし、2つの大きな問題がこの制度の維持を難しくしている。

まず、元々の制度が、日本人の平均寿命は70年、長くて80年ほどの前提で設計されていることだ。しかし、現在新たに誕生した日本人の半分は100歳まで生きると推定される。また60歳を迎えた人の4分の1があと35年、つまり95歳まで生きると思われる。長寿はもちろん良いことだが、人が想定より長い期間年金をもらうことになると、制度の変更も必要となってくる。すでに人口の28%が65歳以上となり、2050年までに33%が65歳以上に達することを考えると、何か手を打つ必要が生じてくる。しかも早急に、だ。

もう一つの問題は、日本の年金が現在でも生活するには不十分であることだ。満額の年間78万円は最低限の生活費としては足りない。国民年金を満額受給している60歳の夫婦が一般的な生活費を賄うには、少なくともさらに月5万円が必要となる。理想的なことを言えば、現在の年金受給者が定年後の生活を賄えるほどの蓄えをしていればいいのだが、日本の金融業界をつかさどる金融庁の調査によると、定年を迎えた人口の半数ほどは、年金以外の収入がない。多くは年金があれば足りると思い、だからこそ40年間コツコツと保険料を支払い続けたのだ。今更彼らにもっと貯蓄をしろと言っても遅い。

Japanese Pensioners

As the fastest aging society in the world, Japan faces a major problem: how to support the retired population. Japan's pension system was established on the assumption that retirees who had paid into the government pension scheme for 40 years would receive a full pension. But two major problems make that promise hard to keep.

First of all, the original plan assumed that people would live until their 70s or perhaps their 80s. But now, half of newborn Japanese can expect to live to be 100. And a fourth of all those who are now 60 years old will still be alive 35 years from now at the age of 95. Living a long and healthy life is generally a good thing, but when it means that people are receiving pensions for more years than expected, some change needs to be made. With 28% of the population now over 65 and estimates of 33% being over 65 by 2050, there is pressure to do something, and it needs to be soon.

A second issue is that Japanese pensions are insufficient even now. A full pension of ¥780,000 per year is insufficient for basic living expenses. A couple in their 60s with a basic government pension would need at least ¥50,000 more per month to meet average household expenses. Ideally the current pensioners would have been saving money over their working years to cover their retirement years. But a survey by the Financial Services Agency (FSA), which regulates Japan's financial industry, has found that half of all retired people had no other source of income beyond their government pension. Many of them had believed that the pension would be enough to live on, so they diligently contributed premiums for 40 years. Now it is too late to tell them to save more.

□ 高齢化　population aging
□ 定年　retirement age
□ 年金制度　pension system
□ 定年退職　compulsory retirement
□ 満額　full amount
□ 支給する　pay
□ 元々の制度　original plan
□ 平均寿命　average life expectancy
□ 前提　assumption
□ 設計されている　designed
□ 想定より長い期間　for more years than expected
□ 何か手を打つ　take action
□ 早急に　as soon as possible
□ 最低限の　minimum
□ 生活費　living expenses
□ 足りない　insufficient
□ 生活費を賄う　meet one's living expenses
□ 年金受給者　pensioner
□ 金融庁　Financial Services Agency
□ コツコツと　diligently
□ 今更〜しても遅い　it is too late to

　それに加えて問題なのは、銀行も郵便局も預貯金に対してほとんど利子を払っていないことだ。1990年代のバブル崩壊以降、日本の投資家は金融リスクを負うことを恐れ、全てを普通預貯金に置いている。いくら蓄財をしたとしても、そのお金がさらにお金を生むことはなく、その間、生活費や医療費はどんどん上がっていく。

　現在の就労人口の保険料を上げる以外に年金基金の不足を補う有効な手立てがない今、国は定年を65歳から70歳に引き上げようとしている。

Added to the problem is the fact that bank and postal savings accounts pay almost zero interest. After the collapse of the bubble in the 1990s, Japanese investors became very nervous about taking any financial risk, so they put their money in regular savings accounts. Whatever savings they may have accumulated, in other words, earns nothing, despite the fact that the cost of living and medical expenses tend to rise.

With few options for solving the pension fund shortage—other than raising premiums for current workers—the government is hoping to raise the retirement age to 70, from the original 65.

□ それに加えて in addition to this

□ バブル崩壊 collapse of the bubble (economy)

□ 金融リスク financial risk

□ 普通預貯金 regular savings account

□ 蓄財する accumulate wealth

□ 就労人口 working population

□ 年金基金 pension fund

□ 有効な手立て effective measures

14

❏ 危険運転

社会

Society

　日本の高齢化が進むにつれ、高齢の自動車運転者も増えている。高齢ドライバーがブレーキとアクセルを踏み間違えたり、シフトレバーをD（ドライブ）ではなくR（リバース）に入れてしまったりして起こる事故が増えると、高齢ドライバーに向けた試験をもっと頻繁に行うべきだという声が高まる。けが人どころか死者まで出してしまう事故を起こす高齢ドライバーがいる中、免許証交付に際して反応時間や視力、判断力の試験は必須とすべきではないだろうか。

　しかし車道や高速道路における最も大きな問題は、高齢ドライバーの問題ではない。2001年の法改正で、今までより重い刑罰が課せられる危険運転致死傷罪が新設された。危険運転の結果、被害者が死亡した場合、最長懲役20年、負傷した場合、最長15年である。

　しかし実際の裁判では、被告人が故意に危険運転を行ったことを立証する責任は検察側にある。2019年広島県で起こった事故では、免許取りたての18歳のドライバーが危険運転致死傷罪の容疑で逮捕された。時速104キロのスピードで車のコントロールを失った。車はガードレールに衝突し、同乗者2名が重傷を負った。同乗者の女性は車から投げ出され脊髄を損傷、両手両足の麻痺が残った。彼女は今も動けない。

　裁判で、被告人はカーブに差し掛かった時にも車をコントロールできると思った、と主張した。弁護団は、被告が車をコントロールすることが難しいということを認識していなかったので、「危険運転」の意図はなかったと主張した。

Dangerous Driving

As Japan's population ages, the number of older drivers has increased. Frequent incidents involving older drivers who step on the accelerator rather than the brake or shift into reverse instead of drive have stimulated calls for more frequent tests for senior drivers. With some senior drivers causing accidents that cause injury and even death, it seems essential that licensing procedures include testing of reaction time, vision, and judgment.

Issues regarding senior drivers are not the biggest problem on the roads and highways. In 2001, a statute was passed that established severe penalties for those who are convicted of malicious driving. The maximum penalty for causing death as a result of dangerous driving was set at 20 years in prison for causing death and 15 years in prison for causing injuries.

But when charges are brought to court, the burden for proving that the indicted driver was willfully reckless is placed on the prosecution. In one case resulting from an accident that occurred in 2019 in Hiroshima prefecture, a newly licensed 18-year-old driver was arrested on suspicion of dangerous driving. He was driving at about 104 kilometers an hour when he lost control of his vehicle. It crashed into a guard rail seriously injuring two passengers. One of the passengers was thrown out of the car, suffered damage to her spinal cord and suffers paralysis in both her arms and legs. She in now unable to move.

At his trial, the driver contended that he thought he could control his vehicle as it went around a bend. The defense took the position that he was not aware that he would have difficulty maintaining control of the vehicle, and therefore could not be charged with "dangerous driving."

□ 免許証交付　issuance of license
□ 反応時間　reaction time
□ 判断力　judgment
□ 法改正　law amendment
□ 刑罰　penalty
□ 危険運転致死傷罪　vehicular homicide
□ 懲役　imprisonment
□ 故意に　willfully
□ 立証する責任　burden of proof
□ 検察　prosecution
□ 容疑　suspicion
□ 同乗者　passenger
□ 脊髄　spinal cord
□ 麻痺　paralysis
□ カーブ　bend
□ 差し掛かる　approaching
□ 弁護団　defense team
□ 認識する　aware

　一方、検察側は、彼が時速150キロほど出していて、同乗者の1人は何度も彼にスピードの出し過ぎを注意したと主張した。被告人が自分の運転が「危険」であったことを「認識」していなかった、という弁護側の主張が成り立つとは到底思えない。どうすれば認識せずにいられたのだろうか。

　また最近、高速道路や一般道で遭遇するのが「あおり運転」と呼ばれる多様な攻撃的運転だ。別の車両の前でわざとスピードを落とす、前の車にピタリと接近する、急ブレーキを踏む、クラクションを鳴らす、頻繁に車線変更を行う、蛇行運転する、また他の車両を無理矢理停止させる、などの行為である。このような恐ろしい行為は、他の車両のドライブレコーダーなどに録画されているが、それによって捕まるリスクがあるにも関わらず、この現象が収まる気配はない。幸い、ドライブレコーダーの映像は法廷でも証拠として採用されている。

The prosecution pointed out that he had sped up to roughly 150 kilometers an hour, and another passenger in the car had repeatedly warned him he was going too fast. It is hard to understand how the defendant's claim that he was "unaware" that his driving was "dangerous" could be presented as a defense. How could his lack of awareness be possible?

Another recent phenomenon on highways and even in city streets is called *aori unten*, which can refer to a variety of aggressive driving behaviors. It may include purposely slowing down in front of another vehicle, tailgating, sudden braking, horn honking, rapidly changing lanes, weaving between lanes, or forcing another vehicle to pull over or stop on the road. These frightening behaviors have been recorded by dash cameras, or drive recorders, in other vehicles, but the fear of being caught in this dangerous activity has not eliminated the phenomena. Fortunately, the drive recorders provide evidence that can be used in court cases.

□到底〜ない　utterly not at all

□遭遇する　encounter

□あおり運転　road rage

□前の車にピタリと接近する　tailgating

□クラクション　horn

□蛇行運転する　weaving between lanes

□現象　phenomenon

□収まる気配はない　no sign of abating

❑ 認知症による徘徊

社会
Society

　社会の高齢化に直面する日本にとって、認知症は深刻な問題である。統計を取り始めた2012年以降、高齢人口の中で、認知症を患う人の数は毎年増加している。

　2020年には、何らかの認知症状を示す日本人で**行方不明**になった人が1万7565人いた。そのうち、74.2%がいなくなったその日のうちに、99.3%が1週間以内に見つかっているが、中には見つからなかったり、発見された時には亡くなっていたりするケースもある。

　全ての**自治体**が備えているわけではないが、中には家からいなくなってしまう人を見つけるための**策を講じている**自治体がある。それらの自治体は、GPS装置を提供することで、警察や保護に動く人たちが、**消息不明**になった人を一刻も早く見つけられるよう手助けしている。

　認知症による**徘徊**で行方不明になった人を見つけ出す難しさは、地域にもよる。都市部の場合、自宅から**徒歩圏内**にいることもあるが、**公共交通機関**を利用して**遠方**に行ってしまい、降りると迷子になり、周りにも顔見知りがいないということが起こる。また地方になると、畑や山林など、車などで**捜索**できないところに迷い込んでしまう。捜索にヘリコプターを使うこともあるが、空からの**視認**には限界がある。捜索には大人数が必要になる。

Wandering Off: Dementia

Dementia is a serious problem in Japan's rapidly aging population. Since the first data became available in 2012, the number of cases of members of the aging population has risen every year.

In 2020, the number of Japanese with some degree of dementia who went missing reached 17,565. While 74.2% of those who had been reported missing were found within the day they disappeared and 99.3% were found within a week, some were either not found or were dead when they were finally located.

Not every municipality is prepared for this problem, but some local governments have implemented strategies to help find those who do wander off from home. These governments have provided global positioning system tracking devices to help police and other rescue units find these people quickly when they go unaccounted for.

When dementia patients do wander off, difficulties in locating them differ depending on the location. In urban areas, they may remain within walking distance of their residence, but they may also board public transportation and travel considerable distances, and when they get off they are lost and no one realizes who they are. In the countryside, they may wander off into fields and forests, where searchers in vehicles cannot easily gain access. Helicopters are often deployed to assist in the search, but there is a limit to visibility from the air. It takes large numbers of searchers on the ground to track them down.

□行方不明になる go missing
□自治体 municipality
□策を講じる take measures
□消息不明 long lost
□徘徊 wander off
□徒歩圏内 within walking distance
□公共交通機関 public transportation
□遠方 distant place
□捜索 search
□視認 visibility

16

❑ 8050問題

社会
Society

　社会と交わることを避ける、今では世界的に知られた日本の「引きこもり」は、通常の社会生活が再び営めるようになること以上の問題を抱えている。10年単位で自室に引きこもることもある彼らは、親に面倒を見てもらっており、その親も年老いてくる。

　引きこもりの問題は今や**新たな局面**を迎えている。引きこもりの中には50代に差しかかる者もいて、その親は80代を迎えている。8050問題とは、親の死後どうやって生活をしていくのかという問題を指す。**内閣府**の調査によると、2015年には54万人ほどの引きこもりがいるという。ただし、これは15歳から39歳の人々だけで、8050問題の**核**となるのは調査の対象ではない40代50代の人々である。

　いくつかの悲劇的な事件では、親が亡くなり、**死体遺棄**の罪で子供が逮捕されている。引きこもりの子供は親の死を前にどう対応したらいいのかわからず、**遺体**をそのまま放置してしまうのだ。

　2015年に施行された**生活困窮者自立支援法**では、このように**困窮している**家族に国が支援の手を差し伸べることができるようにしたが、**申請手続きは容易ではなく**、中には申請手続きを完了する前に諦めてしまう家族もいる。

　また、引きこもりの人たちの**求職支援**を行うプログラムも存在する。しかし、多くの場合これらの仕事は賃金が安い**パート**だったりする。働けるようになっても、そこでいじめに遭う可能性もある。中には事情を理解し、彼らが少しずつ職場になじめるように努める企業もある。このような努力をもっと認めてやらないと、この問題が「9060問題」と名前を変えてしまうかもしれない。

The 8050 Problem

People who withdraw from society, known worldwide now by the Japanese term *hikikomori*, are facing an issue that goes beyond the trying to resume an active life in the outside world. Some who have stayed in the confines of their bedroom for years and even decades are cared for by their parents, and the parents are getting older.

The *hikikomori* problem in Japan has a new twist. Some of these people are entering their 50s just as their parents, on whom they rely almost completely, enter their 80s. The 8050 problem centers on how the children will deal with life after their parents pass away. A government Cabinet Office survey estimates that there are roughly 540,000 *hikikomori* people as of 2015. But that includes only the restricted age group of 15 to 39 year olds. The core of the 8050 problem is those in their 40s and 50s, who were not included in that survey.

In several tragic incidents, a parent has died and the adult "child" has later been arrested for abandoning the corpse, which is a criminal offense. The *hikikomori* child was helpless when it came to dealing with such affairs and simply kept the remains in a room in the house.

The national government passed a law, effective as of 2015, that provides additional welfare payments to families in extreme distress. This would seem to be of help in such cases, but the application process can be challenging, and some of these families simply give up before completion of the filing of a claim.

Some programs assist *hikikomori* people in finding work. The potential downsides are that the job may be part-time and with low pay. The worker may be vulnerable to harassment or bullying, too. But there have been cases where an understanding workplace has enabled such a worker to join the workforce step by step. If more efforts like this are not encouraged, the issue could well be given a new name: the 9060 problem.

□ 引きこもり social withdrawal

□ 新たな局面 new phase

□ 内閣府 Cabinet Office

□ 核 core

□ 死体遺棄 abandonment of a corpse

□ 遺体 corpse

□ 生活困窮者自立支援法 Act on Self-Reliance Support for People in Need

□ 困窮している in distress

□ 申請手続き application process

□ 容易ではない not easy

□ 求職支援 job search assistance

□ パート part-time (work)

17

🔲 最低賃金

これほど最低賃金が低い日本において、パートタイマーや**非正規労働者**がどうやって生活しているのか不思議だ。2020年度の最低賃金は驚愕の1円増しという時給901円から902円への引き上げだった。これが平均だ。秋田や鳥取を含む16県では、これまで最低時給が800円を下回っていた。2021年に28円の増額が実行され、最も低かった7県の最低時給がついに820円となり、全国平均は930円となった。政府は「より早期に」全国平均を1,000円まで引き上げたいと言っている。しかし、それに成功しても、労働者にとってまともな生活ができるほどの稼ぎにはならない。

コロナ禍の悪影響にも関わらず、米国や欧州では2020年に5%ほど賃金が上昇し、2021年には2%から4%の上昇が見られた。**日本商工会議所**は政府に対して2021年の最低賃金の**据え置き**を要望した。なぜか。商工会議所は、コロナ禍のせいで中小企業は厳しい状況に置かれており、賃金を引き上げると**存続**できないという。企業が優先されるのだ。

しかし、最低3%の引き上げを主張する者は、**生産性**の低い、出来の悪いビジネスモデルを持つ企業が、安い労働力に頼ることを許してはいけないと訴える。低賃金を含む古い習慣に**しがみつく**商売の仕方を変えなければいけない、と。最低賃金を上げることで、サービス業で働く労働者の意欲が向上し、**個人消費**も促すことで経済全体が**活気づく**と彼らは主張する。

The Minimum Wage

It is hard to understand how part-time and irregular workers in Japan survive given that the minimum wage is so low. Japan's minimum hourly wage in fiscal 2020 rose an astoundingly miserable ¥1 from ¥901 to ¥902. This is the average. Sixteen prefectures including Akita and Tottori previously had minimum hourly wages below ¥800. With an increase of ¥28 in 2021, the minimum hourly wage in the seven lowest paying prefectures is finally ¥820 and the national average is ¥930. The government says it wants to raise the national figure to ¥1,000 "as soon as possible." Even if it succeeds in doing that, workers will not be paid enough to earn a decent living.

Despite the negative impact of the coronavirus pandemic, the United States and Europe raised their wages by approximately 5% in 2020 and by between 2% and 4% in 2021. The Japan Chamber of Commerce and Industry has asked the government to allow businesses to make no increase in the minimum wage for 2021. Why? The organization claims that smaller businesses are struggling due to the coronavirus crisis. Increase wages, it says, and many of those companies will not survive. It puts the companies first.

Supporters of an increase of at least 3%, however, say that companies with poor business models yielding poor productivity should not be allowed to continue to depend on cheap labor. They have to change the way they do business instead of clinging to old patterns, including low wages. These supporters say that raising the minimum wage would help the whole economy, provide motivation for workers in the services sector, and boost private consumption.

□非正規労働者　irregular worker
□まともな生活　decent living
□日本商工会議所　the Japan Chamber of Commerce and Industry
□据え置き　deferment
□存続する　survive
□生産性　productivity
□～にしがみつく　cling to
□個人消費　private consumption
□活気づく　become lively

社会

Society

❑ 非正規雇用

「日本資本主義の父」渋沢栄一の事業理念は、商売は利益を追求するが、同時に売り手、買い手、社会全てが恩恵にあずからなければならないというものだ。理想的に言うと、それには株主のみならず、従業員を加えた全てのステークホルダーが含まれる。

ある意味、日本の商売は職場の安定を提供し、手堅く労働力を維持してきたと言える。それを可能にした要因がいくつか存在する。一つは減少を続ける労働人口。もう一つは雇用主が正社員に対して誠実であること。しかしそれは、企業側が短期間しか雇用しない従業員を増やすことで成り立っている。彼らはいわゆる「サラリーマン」のように守られていない。

非正規雇用の従業員は1990年の20%から2021年には40%近くまで増加した。例外はあるものの、大体は若い女性であり、彼女らは特に訓練を必要としない単純な仕事を与えられた。そういった従業員の中には特殊な技能や経験を職場にもたらす者もいるが、会社への貢献に対する見返りはない。企業は安い賃金しか払わず、契約期間が終わればそれまでだ。このやり方に対して渋沢がなんと言うか聞いてみたいものだ。

子供がある程度大きくなったら職場復帰を希望する女性を、政府は有効活用したいと言うが、プロ意識の高い母親たちは職場に戻ることにも苦労する。職場復帰したある女性は当初、子供の世話をするため週15時間の勤務とした。彼女は新人扱いされ、ソニーやNHKなど大手企業の人事部での19年に及ぶキャリアがあるにもかかわらず、リサイクルの袋の整理を命じられた。さらに問題となったのは、以前の仕事と比較して時給が4割に減少となったことだ。最終的には昇進して給料も上がり正社員と同じ条件で働けるようになったが、彼女のようなケースは日本の職場ではまだまれだ。

66

"Non-regular" Workers

The business philosophy of the "father of Japanese business," Eiichi Shibusawa, holds that business should pursue profits, but should benefit buyers, sellers, and society. Ideally that would include all stakeholders—not just stockholders—such as employees.

In part, Japanese businesses have offered job security and maintained a stable labor force. But they have been able to do so as a result of several factors. One is the shrinking labor force. Another is that employers are loyal to their core workers. But they have done that by hiring more employees on short-term contracts. These people have very few of the protections given to the so-called salarymen.

These "non-regular" workers have increased from 20% in 1990 to almost 40% in 2021. Often, but not exclusively, young and female, these workers are not just doing just simple tasks that require little training. Some bring special abilities and experience to the workplace, but they are not rewarded for their contributions to the company. The company pays them low wages and when they get to the end of their contract, they are simply let go. It would be interesting to hear Shibusawa's take on this process.

Despite the government's expressed desire to take advantage of women who want to return to the workplace after their children reach a certain age, professionally minded mothers struggle to ease back into the workplace. One workplace returnee took a job working just 15 hours a week so that she could care for her child. She was treated as a beginner and assigned to organize bags for recycling, despite having 19 years of experience working in human resources for major employers including Sony and NHK. Topping off the problem was the fact that her initial hourly wage was only 40% of what she had earned at her last job. Eventually she was promoted, given a pay raise, and received the same benefits as a full-time employee. But she is a rarity in the Japanese workplace.

□事業理念　business philosophy
□利益を追求する　pursue profits
□恩恵にあずかる　enjoy the benefit
□株主　stockholder
□職場の安定　job security
□手堅く　steady
□要因　factor
□いわゆる　so-called
□サラリーマン　office worker
□従業員　worker
□技能　skill
□貢献　contribution
□見返り　reward
□有効活用　effective use
□プロ意識　professional awareness
□当初　at first
□人事部　human resources department
□命じられた　ordered
□比較して　compared to
□昇進する　get promoted

渋沢栄一
Eiichi Shibusawa

男女平等や全ての従業員を同じように扱うことを推進する厳しい法律がさらに重要となってくる。日本の労働人口は減少している。現在の雇用制度を再検討し、働きたい人が働けるように制度を見直す必要がある。これには渋沢も賛成するだろう。

Tougher laws promoting gender equality and equal treatment of all types of employees will be increasingly important. Japan faces a declining workforce. It is time to reexamine the system of employment and make adjustments so that people who want to work can do so. Shibusawa would approve.

□男女平等　gender equality

□雇用制度　employment system

□再検討する　reexamine

19

□ ケアワーカーの低賃金

社会
Society

　総理大臣などが女性を「輝かせる」とか職場復帰を促すなどと言うと、ほとんどの日本人がまず思い浮かべるのは、それは実際どういう意味なのだろうか、という疑問である。女性が子供や年老いた親を「ワンオペ」で面倒見ている状況で、フルタイムの仕事は難しいのではないだろうか。「輝かせる」とは、正社員としての同等の賃金ではなく、要するに低賃金でパートの仕事に就くことを意味するのではないかとうがった見方をしてしまう。

　この問題の明暗を分けるのは、自宅か職場の近くに保育所があるかどうかだ。もしも信頼できる保育所に子供を預けることができれば、親は子供が安全に面倒を見てもらえていると安心していられる。

　人の寿命が延びるにつれて、働く世代が親の面倒も見なければならなくなる可能性も高くなっている。これはこれで、いろいろ問題がある。

　では、こういったケアワーカーたちの面倒を見るのは誰なのだろうか。子供や老人の面倒を見るという仕事自体はとても充実していると感じるかもしれない。何よりも自分で自分のことができない人を手伝うわけだから。しかし、このような善意の心に対する対価があまりにも小さい。彼らは月に20万円程度しかもらえない。そのような給料で、彼らはどうやって生計を立てているのだろうか。国も、このような介護や保育施設を運営する事業所も、彼らの給料を倍にするべきだ。民間企業は、そんなに給料を上げたらビジネスが立ち行かないと文句を言うだろう。それならば、そもそもそのようなビジネスモデルに問題がある。弱者の面倒を見る負担を低賃金で働く従業員に背負わせてはならない。国は社会保障の一環として、このような施設の補助を行わなければならない。

Poor Pay for Care-providers

When prime ministers talk about helping women "shine" or enabling them to return to work, one of the first question that most Japanese ask is what that really means. With women handling *wan-ope* (single-operator) care for their own children or for their elderly parents, it is hard to see how they can handle full-time employment as well. One suspects, of course, that "shining" actually means taking part-time work at low pay, not equal pay for regular employment.

The tripwire for this issue is the availability of regular child-care facilities near the home or the workplace. If dependable child-care were available, then a parent could rest assured that his or her child was safe and well looked after.

With people living longer now, there is a greater possibility that the working population will also have to take care of their parents. That presents its own issues.

Who cares for the care-providers? It would at least seem that people who take care of children or senior citizens find their work rewarding. After all, they are helping people who are not able to act independently. But the pay offered to these kind souls is pitiful. If they only receive a monthly pay of ¥200,000 or so, how can they themselves survive? The government and the businesses that run these care centers need to double the salaries of these employees. Private business owners are likely to moan that they can't continue operating if they increase the pay of their employees. Well, if that is the case, their business model isn't sustainable. They should not put the burden of care-giving on the backs of poorly paid employees. The government should certainly subsidize these facilities as part of the social welfare system.

□輝かせる　make someone shine

□促す　encourage

□ワンオペ　one-person-operator

□うがった見方　look at things from a biased viewpoint

□この問題の明暗を分ける　decide the outcome of the issue

□保育所　child-care facilities

□世代　generation

□善意の心　kind souls

□対価　compensation

□生計を立てる　make a living

□介護　care

□事業所　place of business

□負担を背負わせる　put the burden

□社会保障　social welfare

□一環として　as part of

□補助　subsidize

71

20

❏ リモートワーク

　新型コロナウイルスによるパンデミックは、ビジネス界にいろいろな形で影響を及ぼした。間違いなく最も大きな影響は、少なくとも週のうち数日はリモートで仕事をするようになったことだ。もちろん、これを実現するには安定したブロードバンドネットワークが必要になる。会社のデータベースにログインして、Zoomなどのアプリで会議を行っている会社員にとって、技術的トラブルや接続が切れることは一大事である。

　会社員にとってリモートワークの利点は、満員電車での長時間の通勤のストレスから解放されることだ。人混みの中での感染リスクを防げるならば尚更だ。会社員は少しだけ長く寝ていられるし、仕事を始めるまでの時間を少しだけ長く確保でき、服装も普段着でよく、会社のエレベーターで嫌な同僚に会うこともない。もしかしたら最も大きな利点は、常に鳴り続けて仕事を中断させる電話に出る必要がないことかもしれない。

　欠点は家に缶詰めになってしまうことだ。同じく終日家にいる子供がいれば、自分の仕事をこなしながら、子供の要求に応えなくてはならない。先に述べたような「会社」への不満もあるが、ランチに一緒に行くなど同僚とのたわいのないやりとりがないことを寂しくも思う。

　この状況がもたらした好機の一つは、上司の役割や生産性の目標などを見直す機会となったことだ。単に職場に長くいることで社員の生産性を評価することができないので、上司は部下が真面目に働いていることを評価する別の方法を考えなければならない。このような状況で生産性に変化が出るかどうか、とても興味深い。もしも従業員が就業時間内にそれぞれの仕事に集中できるのであれば、従来のように終日会社で過ごす日常に戻さなくてもよくなるかもしれない。もしも部下が目の前にいなかったら、上司はどうやって管理するのか。

Remote Work

The COVID-19 pandemic has influenced the business world in many ways. Undoubtedly the largest impact has been the switch to working remotely at least some weekdays. Doing this requires, of course, a stable broadband internet connection. Any technical failure or a break in the connection can cause major problems for workers logging into their company databases or holding meetings on platforms such as Zoom.

The upside for most employees is the reduction in stress that results from long commutes on crowded trains, especially with the potential spread of the virus in crowds. Workers can sleep a bit longer, take a little more time getting ready to start work, dress casually, and avoid irritating coworkers in the elevators at the office. Perhaps the most positive advantage is not having their work interrupted by constant phone calls during the day.

The downside is being stuck at home all day. If they have children who are also at home all day, then they have to deal with their own work and their children's demands. And despite their previous complaints about "the office," they miss the camaraderie of friends at work and going out to lunch together.

One of the opportunities that this situation has brought about is a chance to reexamine managers' roles and productivity goals. Simply being "at work" for long hours is no longer a way of evaluating an employee's productivity, so managers have to find another way of evaluating how hard they are working. It will be interesting to see whether productivity changes under these circumstances. If workers can concentrate on their jobs during remote business hours, there may be no reason to return to in-office routines on a full-time basis. And if subordinates are not right in front of them, how will managers manage?

□接続が切れる　break in the connection
□利点　advantage
□人混み　crowd of people
□尚更だ　all the more
□家に缶詰めになる　be stuck at home
□終日　all day
□たわいのない　innocent, trivial
□好機　good opportunity
□評価する　evaluate
□就業時間　working hours
□終日会社で過ごす日常　in-office routines on a full-time basis

　たとえ規制が緩和されて出社する機会が増えたとしても、もう一つ問題が残っている。週に何日出社すればいいのだろうか。すでに、会社員は少なくとも週に1日は会社以外の場所にいることを希望する、という推測もある。**非公式の調査**などでは、水曜日が**最有力候補**だ。とは言っても、大多数の人にとって自宅にいて一人で働くことは**あまりにも寂しく**、親交を深めるためにも会社員は定期的には出社したいと思うだろう。

　職場環境がどのように変わるか予測するのは難しいが、少なくとも以前の「普通」に完全に戻ることはないと言えるだろう。

Even when restrictions are eventually lifted and in-office work becomes more common, there is another issue to consider: how many days a week should people go to the office? Already there is speculation that employees will want at least one day a week away from the office. The leading candidate according to informal surveys say Wednesdays are appealing. On the other hand, working at home is just too lonely for the majority, so employees probably will want to come to their offices at least once in a while, for the camaraderie.

While it is hard to predict exactly how things in the workplace will change, it is safe to say that there will not be a full return to the previous "normal."

□非公式の　informal

□最有力候補　leading candidate

□あまりにも寂しい　just too lonely

❏ ふるさと回帰

社会
Society

21

　長きにわたる**人口動態上の傾向**として、若い人は田舎を後にして、仕事やその他の機会を求めて都会に向かった。地方から東京、大阪、その他都市部に向かう人口は常に増えていった。首都圏では人口が増える一方、地方の集落は高齢化や**過疎化**が進んだ。しかし、新型コロナ禍で就業形態が多様化する以前から、一部の都会での生活者は逆方向に動き始めていた。

　数十年さかのぼれば、ゆっくり過ごす田舎生活を求めてごみごみした都会を離れて行くのは、定年退職後の人々だった。彼らは主に生まれ育った地に戻って行く。しかし、今では若者や、地方に**縁もゆかりもない人**など、従来と違うタイプの人々が、地方への移住を支援するNGO団体、**ふるさと回帰支援センター**に連絡してくるようになった。最近では、香川、山梨、愛媛、福島の市町村も、そのような人々を取り込むべく積極的に活動し始めた。地元を**活性化**させようと、転入者の受け入れに積極的な自治体などが企画するプロジェクトを、NGOでは宣伝する活動を行っている。

　自らの人生を見直し、より平和で静かな、物価も安いライフスタイル、より良いワークライフバランス、さらには地元コミュニティへの参加を求める若者のお陰で、地方への興味が高まっている。

　「移民」である彼らの中には自ら仕事を持ってくる者もいる。安定したブロードバンドのインターネットサービスが提供されていれば、主な仕事をオンラインでこなせるし、人混みを避け、狭いアパートから職場への長時間の通勤を**回避**することができる。彼らはデバイスのスイッチを入れればどこででも仕事ができる。信頼できる宅配便があれば必要な**機材**や**資材**など、都会の業者からなんでも翌日までに**取り寄せる**ことができる。

Country Roads toward Home

One long-term Japanese demographic trend has been for young people to leave the rural areas behind and head to the cities for jobs and other opportunities. Net emigration from the countryside to Tokyo, Osaka, and other urban centers has risen consistently. The metropolitan areas have steadily climbed while rural communities have aged and depopulated. But even before the COVID pandemic and remote work options arrived, some city-dwellers had begun to head in the opposite direction.

In earlier decades, it was retired people who left crowded urban areas for the slower country life, and often they were returning to their childhood homes. But now other people—younger and without local connections—are contacting the NGO Furusato Kaiki Shien Center which supports people who want to move to rural areas. Recent outreach efforts have been made from towns in Kagawa, Yamanashi, Ehime, and Fukushima prefectures. This organization helps advertise projects that are eager and willing to accept new residents to revitalize their local communities.

Interest in rural areas has been boosted by young people re-evaluating their lives, looking for peace and quiet, a cheaper lifestyle, a better work-life balance, and perhaps participation in a local community.

Some of these "migrants" bring their jobs with them. If there is dependable broadband internet service available, those who do most of their work online can avoid crowds and a long daily commute from a cramped apartment to a workplace. They can turn on their devices anywhere and be ready to work. Dependable delivery services allow overnight deliveries of necessary equipment, supplies, and devices, and also guarantee access to almost anything one could want from urban distributors.

　それ以外_{いがい}にも、仕事_{しごと}に不満_{ふまん}を抱_{かか}え農業_{のうぎょう}に**従事_{じゅうじ}する**ために移住_{いじゅう}する者_{もの}もいる。彼_{かれ}らは地元民_{じもとみん}からいろいろ教_{おし}えてもらうことが多_{おお}い。他_{ほか}にも伝統技術_{でんとうぎじゅつ}の継承_{けいしょう}のために、若_{わか}い人_{ひと}が都会_{とかい}へ出_でてしまったことで**途絶_{とだ}えて**しまいそうな技術_{ぎじゅつ}を守_{まも}るべく、力_{ちから}を注_{そそ}ぐ者_{もの}もいる。

　この傾向_{けいこう}は、**消滅_{しょうめつ}**に向_むかっていた集落_{しゅうらく}や村_{むら}にとっては**朗報_{ろうほう}**だ。例_{たと}えば、四国_{しこく}の四万十町_{しまんとちょう}では、移住者_{いじゅうしゃ}に住宅_{じゅうたく}や子育_{こそだ}て支援_{しえん}を提供_{ていきょう}している。新_{あたら}しい住民_{じゅうみん}たちは、田舎_{いなか}であるがゆえのインフラ不足_{ぶそく}に対_{たい}して大_{おお}きな不満_{ふまん}はないようだ。むしろ、彼_{かれ}らは親切_{しんせつ}な地元_{じもと}コミュニティや地域_{ちいき}に**属_{ぞく}している**感覚_{かんかく}に惹_ひかれている。

Other migrants have left unsatisfying occupations and have taken up farming, often with the tutoring of local people who are willing to help. Still others have devoted their energies to learning traditional crafts, preventing those skills from disappearing due to the out-migration of young people.

This trend is encouraging to receiving towns and villages who once seemed headed for extinction. The sparsely populated town of Shimanto, in the island of Shikoku, for example, offers subsidies for housing and child care for the newly arrived. It seems that the new residents are undeterred by the lack of infrastructure in the countryside. Instead they are attracted by the helpfulness of the local community and the sense of belonging to a neighborhood.

□〜に従事する　engage in

□途絶える　cease to exist

□消滅　extinction

□朗報　good news

□〜であるがゆえの　because of

□〜に属する　belong to

□〜に惹かれている　be attracted by

22

❑ 人口減少
じんこうげんしょう

日本のメディアも政府も、人口減少を問題視するのに**躍起**になっているようだ。

若い人が都会での仕事や他の魅力的なことを求めて地方を離れると、地元の学校では生徒が減る。大人が近くの町で仕事をすると、**畑は放置される**。小さな町がさらに小さくなると、機器も人材もそろった病院で医療を受けるために他の町と協力せざるを得なくなる。そして、地方の人口が減れば、土地はイノシシやクマ、サルに**占拠されて**しまう。

しかし、人口が減れば、日本はより住みやすい国になるかもしれない。例えば、朝のラッシュ時に乗客が電車や地下鉄でゆっくり座れるとしたらどうだろう。**連休**時の高速道路の30キロにも及ぶ**渋滞**がなくなったらどうだろう。住宅街でも、コンクリートが減って木々が増えたらどうだろう。

出生率が上がらなければ、日本の人口は現在の1.26億人から2060年までに9000万人に減ると予測されている。確かに**半世紀**後の話だが、予測はそうなっている。それは人が思うほど恐ろしい予測ではないのではないか。**人口密度**が下がれば、日本はもっと住みやすくなるかもしれない。

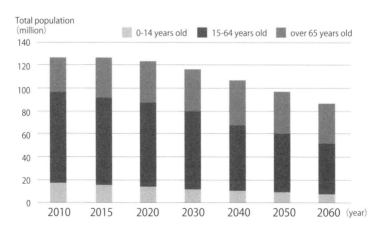

Estimated future population of Japan
(Ministry of Internal Affairs and Communications, National Institute of Population and Social Security Research)

年齢区分別将来人口推計（データ出典：総務省および国立社会保障・人口問題研究所）

Shrinking Population

The Japanese media and government seem determined to make depopulation a cause for concern.

When young people leave the countryside to find jobs and other attractions in the urban areas, it leaves the local schools without enough students. When adults take jobs in nearby towns, it leaves the fields unattended. When small towns grow smaller, they have to somehow cooperate with other towns in order to maintain sufficient medical care in hospitals with enough equipment and staff members. And when the human population in the countryside shrinks, the land will be turned over to the wild boars, the bears, and the monkeys.

With a smaller population, however, Japan could become a more livable country. Consider the appeal of a morning rush hour with commuters actually sitting down during their ride to work on the trains and subways. Consider the highways without 30-kilometer backed-up traffic during long annual holidays. Consider urban residential areas with less concrete and more trees between the buildings.

It is predicted that unless the birthrate increases, Japan's population will drop from roughly 126 million today to 90 million by 2060. Admittedly that is a half-century in the future, but that's the prediction. And it's not as frightening a prospect as some people would like us to think. Japan might actually be a nicer place to live if the population density were lower.

□躍起になる　be desperate to

□畑は放置される　leave the fields unattended

□イノシシ　wild boar

□～に占拠される　be taken over by

□連休　consecutive holidays

□渋滞　congestion

□出生率　birthrate

□半世紀　a half-century

□人口密度　population density

エネルギー・環境

<ruby>環境<rt>かんきょう</rt></ruby>

Energy and Environment

23

❏ 福島原発事故の余波

　2011年3月11日の**東日本大震災**と大津波から丸10年が過ぎた。マグニチュード9.0の地震と、それがもたらした大津波も十分ひどいが、福島第一原発の破壊はいまだに解決されない多くの問題を日本に残している。

　放射能汚染のために**避難を余儀なくされた**第一原発近くの住民にとって、**直近の問題**は自分たちの家に戻れる日が来るのかどうかである。**帰還して定住できる可能性は限りなく低い**。とはいえ、政府の建てた**仮設住宅**に住んでいる場合、いつまでも住み続けるわけにもいかない。また全てを失った人々の子供を政府はいつまで援助してくれるのだろうか。

　避難した人々は日本中の新しい土地で新しい生活や仕事を始めることを強いられた。新しい学校に転校した子供たちは、**被ばくしている**かもしれないと、**いじめの対象となった**。

　メルトダウンがいまだに問題であることは明白だ。メルトダウンの規模は原子力事故に際して用いられる国際的な基準で最も高いレベル7。1986年の**チェルノブイリ原発事故**と同レベルだ。この2つのケース以外に、この最高レベルに分類された事故はない。

　放射線量の高さから大熊町や双葉町など7つの市町村が**帰還困難区域**に指定されている。事故直後と比較すると、当時の3割まで減少したが、それでも相当大きな区域で、東京23区の半分程度の面積である。いつ解除されるか誰にもわからないが、もう誰もそこに住むことができないことは間違いない。

福島第一原子力発電所事故
Fukushima No.1 Nuclear
Power Plant Accident

Fukushima Disaster Aftereffects

A full decade has passed since the Great East Japan Earthquake and tsunami on March 11, 2011. The magnitude 9.0 quake and the resulting tsunami were bad enough, but the destruction of the Fukushima No. 1 nuclear power plant has left Japan with a number of serious issues still unsolved.

Of immediate concern to those who lived near the plant and were forced to evacuate due to nuclear contamination is whether they will ever be able to return to their original homes. Their chances of a permanent return are minimal. On the other hand, if they are living in housing provided by the government for evacuees, they will not be able to live there forever. And how long will the government support the children of those who have lost everything?

Those who have evacuated have been forced to establish new lives and to take new jobs in different parts of the country. Children in new schools have faced bullying as a result of their possible exposure to nuclear contamination.

It is clear that the meltdown is an ongoing problem. The plant meltdown is ranked 7, the highest level, in terms of an internationally recognized scale of the severity of nuclear crises. That puts it at the same level as the 1986 Chernobyl disaster. No other accidents have been classified as high as these two.

Due to high radiation levels seven towns including Okuma and Futaba remain no-go zones. This is 30% of the largest designated zone immediately after the disaster, but it is a sizable area, roughly half the size of Tokyo's 23 wards. No one knows when the entry ban will be removed, but it is certain that no one will be able to reside there again.

□東日本大震災　Great East Japan Earthquake

□避難を余儀なくされる　be forced to evacuate

□直近の問題　immediate concern

□帰還する　return home

□限りなく低い　minimal

□仮設住宅　temporary housing

□被ばくしている　exposure to nuclear contamination

□いじめの対象となる　subject to bullying

□～に際して　at the time of

□用いられる　be used

□チェルノブイリ原発事故　1986 Chernobyl disaster

□放射線量　radiation dose

□帰還困難区域　no-go zone

東京電力は、原発を完全に解体するのに2051年までかかると言う。しかし、多くの専門家は、その期日はあくまでも理想であって、現実的ではないと指摘する。

明白な脅威は、原発周辺の広大な土地に設置されたタンク内の、放射性物質を含む処理済み汚染水だ。事故から10年たった時点で、原発の敷地内で124万トンの汚染水がタンクに保管されている。その水には低放射性物質のトリチウムが含まれている。原子炉を冷やし続けるために必要な大量の水によって生じるものだ。タンクは施設内の広大な土地に設置されているが、その土地も2022年秋には満杯になると推定されている。東京電力も政府もどうするか決めかねている。

その水を太平洋に流して大丈夫なのだろうか。政府はこの選択をしようとしている。比較的低容量のトリチウム以外の汚染物質は、海に流す前に取り除くことができると主張する。

しかし、現状でも14の国と地域は福島県産物に輸入規制をかけている。さらに、汚染物質を海に放出すれば、規制も強化されるだろう。地元の漁師たちはこの10年間、生活を立て直すのに苦労してきた。福島県産の水産物が再び受け入れられ始めた矢先に、汚染水が海に放出されれば、福島ブランドがまた被害を受けることを彼らは当然のことながら恐れる。

原発事故から10年がたち、日本ではより厳しい安全基準を満たしたはずの原子炉が9つ再稼働した。うち7基は現在稼働している。その他26基は稼働に向けて申請手続きが取られている。福島原発の6基を含む合計26基が廃炉の予定である。その裏には不都合な真実がある。日本国中どこを探しても放射性廃棄物を貯蔵できる安全な場所などないのだ。

TEPCO has estimated that decommissioning the entire facility will continue through 2051. But many experts think that timetable is more hopeful than realistic.

The obvious threat is the accumulating nuclear-contaminated water that now fills tanks in huge fields surrounding the disaster site. At the time of the tenth anniversary of the disaster, there were already 1.24 million tons of contaminated water in tanks on the premises of the plant. That water is contaminated with low-toxic radioactive tritium. It comes from the massive amounts of water that are necessary in cooling the reactors. The tanks now cover a huge space around the facility, and it is estimated that space may run out by autumn of 2022. Neither TEPCO nor the government have decided what to do with it.

Can that water be safely released into the Pacific? This is the option that the government is leaning toward. It claims that most of the contaminants, except the relatively low toxic tritium, can be removed prior to releasing it into the Pacific.

But 14 countries and regions currently restrict imports from Fukushima as it is. Any further release of such contaminants will surely increase restrictions. Local fishers have struggled to earn a living for the past decade. Just as they are beginning to see a bit of improvement in acceptance of Fukushima products, they naturally fear that the Fukushima brand will be heavily damaged by dumping this water into the ocean.

Ten years after the disaster, nine reactors in Japan have been restarted with hopefully stricter safety standards in place. Of these, seven are in operation. Another 26 are currently undergoing the approval process. A total of 26 reactors, including the six at the Fukushima No. 1 nuclear power plant are to be decommissioned. In the background of all this is one very inconvenient truth: there is no safe place in Japan to put any nuclear waste.

□東京電力　Tokyo Electric Power Company; TEPCO

□原発を解体する　dismantle the nuclear power plant

□脅威　threat

□低放射性物質　low radioactive material

□満杯になる　become full

□低容量の　low volume

□汚染物質　contaminant

□輸入規制　import restrictions

□生活を立て直す　rebuild one's life

□水産物　marine products

□矢先に　just as

□当然のことながら　naturally

□再稼働する　resume operations

□稼働している　in operation

□廃炉　decommissioning a nuclear reactor

□不都合な真実　inconvenient truth

□放射性廃棄物　nuclear waste

87

❑ 続く原発依存

2021年6月、関西電力（KEPCO）は福井県の美浜原発3号機を再稼働した。KEPCOも地元企業も、大阪や**地元産業**には電力が必要だと主張した。しかし、再稼働を決めた論理は理解し難い。

まず、日本の原発の一般的な**耐用年数**は40年と定められていた。しかし、新たな原発を作ることに対して世論の同意を得るのが難しいと考え、政府は原発の運転期間を最長で60年超に延長することを検討し始めた。**与党自民党**や経済界の一部も新しい原発を建設するより**既存**のものを使う方が簡単だと言う。しかし、国民は古い原発を使い続けることの安全性**を危惧**し、中でも過去に事故を起こした原発に対して不安を覚える。

福井の美浜原発3号機は、特別ルールに基づく原子力委員会の認可を受けて44年目に再稼働した。今までの**規制破り**や見逃しの**前歴**を考えると、たとえもっと「若い」原発であっても再稼働の安全性を信頼することは難しい。KEPCOは、福島で起こった大地震と津波により引き起こされた東電（TEPCO）の福島第一原発の爆発という大災害から一体何を学んだのだろうか？

さらにあの**老朽化**した原発の**認可が下りた経緯**も不透明だ。一つ明確だったのは、再稼働の認可に必要な地元の同意を得やすくするべく**交付金**が支給されたことだ。実際、福井県知事が再稼働に同意する前に、地元に対して25億円が交付されることが決まった。

Continuing Nuclear-power Dependency

In June 2021, Kansai Electric Power Company (KEPCO) rebooted its No. 3 reactor in the Mihama nuclear power station in Fukui Prefecture. Osaka and its industries need power, said the company and local businesses. But the logic of the decision to restart the reactor was hard to grasp.

First of all, the standard approved lifetime of a nuclear reactor in Japan was once set at 40 years. But now Japan is considering extending the maximum service period beyond 60 years due to the anticipated public opposition to construction of any new plants. The ruling Liberal Democratic Party and some business circles contend that extending the use of current plants is easier than building new ones. The public, however, has shown concerns about the safety of aging reactors, especially those that have previously had accidents.

Mihama No. 3 was restarted in its 44th year by special approval from the governing agency. Given the poor record of failings in regulation and oversight, one could hardly be confident that this restart would be safe, even in a "younger" reactor. Had KEPCO learned much from the Tokyo Electric Power Company (TEPCO) disaster in Fukushima, where an earthquake and tsunami knocked out the Fukushima No. 1 nuclear power station?

Further, there was a lack of transparency about how permission was given for the old reactor. It was clear, however, that subsidies were provided to sweeten local opinion in order to get the reboot approval. In fact, a subsidy of ¥2.5 billion to local communities was agreed upon before the governor of Fukui prefecture agreed to the restart.

□地元産業　local industry
□耐用年数　service life
□与党　ruling party
□自民党　Liberal Democratic Party
□既存の　existing
□〜を危惧する　be concerned about
□規制破り　failing in regulation
□見逃し　oversight
□前歴　prior history
□老朽化した　deteriorated
□認可が下りる　approval is granted
□経緯　circumstance
□交付金　subsidy

福島の災害や福井の老朽化した施設の問題がある中、日本のエネルギー安全保障の課題は大きくのしかかる。福島の事故以前は、電力の約30%を原発が担っていた。それが今では約6%だ。不足分を補うべく、海外から燃料を輸入している。燃料の輸送にも火力発電にも二酸化炭素が生じる。日本はパリ協定の合意に基づき、2030年までに2013年の水準から排出量を26%削減すると公約している。

　日本のような資源に乏しい国が原子力を止めるのは難しい。原発ならCO$_2$排出なしに常時電力を供給できるのだから。海外から燃料をほとんど輸入する必要もない。洋上風力発電や太陽光発電の施設ほど土地も必要ない。しかし、35%の日本人は原発をなくしてほしいと思っている。原子力発電にまつわる議論は、今後も長く続くであろう。

Despite the issues of the Fukushima disaster and the restart of the aged Fukui facility, the issue of energy security looms large. Until the Fukushima disaster, some 30% of Japan's power came from nuclear plants. That figure is now roughly 6%. To make up for this shortage, more fuel must be brought from overseas. Both the transportation of the fuel and the burning of it produce carbon dioxide, and Japan has promised to lower emissions 26% from 2013 levels by 2030 under its commitments to the Paris Accord.

Nuclear power is hard for a resource-limited nation like Japan to surrender. It produces carbon-free power nonstop. It requires very little fuel imports from overseas. It takes up little land, in contrast with onshore wind turbines and solar energy farms. But some 39% of Japanese people want to see all nuclear plants closed. The debate over nuclear power is far from over.

□エネルギー安全保障　energy security

□大きくのしかかる　loom large

□不足分を補うべく　to make up for this shortage

□二酸化炭素　carbon dioxide

□パリ協定　Paris Accord

□排出量　emission

□資源に乏しい　resource-limited

□洋上風力発電　offshore wind power generation

□〜にまつわる　related to

❑ 太陽光発電

25

すでに50年以上、日本の中でも気候の良い緯度に位置する住宅では、太陽光で水を温めるためにソーラーパネルを屋根に設置してきた。新しいソーラーパネル「ファーム」が、エネルギーを蓄電するために遊休農地やビルの屋上、山肌などに現れ始めた。

これらのパネルによって日本の原発依存を解消できるのだろうか。たぶん無理だろう。まずは、ソーラーパネルによって供給できるエネルギー量の割合の問題がある。実際、その割合は小さい。また天候に依存する問題がある。終日太陽が出ない日があれば、エネルギーは電池に蓄えられない。当然、夜には役に立たない。

次に、電池が現在高額であり、決して環境に優しいとはいえない素材に依存することがある。レアアースに依存する電池はそれ自体が脅威だ。

最後に、パネルの経年劣化の問題がある。「クリーンエネルギー」は魅力的だが、パネルはいずれ老朽化し、日本はまた別の環境問題を抱えることになる。パネルは再利用できず、恒久的に廃棄できる安全な場所はない。

❑ プラスチック

26

もう何十年もの間、外国人の居住者や観光客はデパートなどで見受けられる日本の過剰包装に言及してきた。全ての購入品が段ボール、紙、プラスチックなどで何重にも包装され、その包装のほとんどが廃棄されてしまうかリサイクルされる。幸いにもその時代は過ぎ、今では店でも包装の簡素化が進んでいる。中でもプラスチックの利用がそれに該当する。

Solar Energy

For over a half-century, houses in the sunnier latitudes of Japan have used solar roof panels to absorb daytime sunshine for heating water. Now solar panel "farms" are appearing in disused fields, on building rooftops, and on mountain slopes gathering power to be stored in batteries for many other uses as well.

Are these panels a way of reducing Japan's dependence on nuclear power? Probably not. First there is the issue of the percentage of electricity needs that solar panels can supply. In actual fact, that percentage is comparatively small. And they depend on the weather. When there is no sunshine during the day, there is no energy to store in batteries. At night, of course, they are ineffective.

Second, the batteries are currently expensive and dependent on materials that are not particularly environmentally friendly. Batteries that depend on rare earths are a threat all of their own.

Finally, there is the issue of the aging panels. "Clean energy" is appealing, but eventually the panels will deteriorate and Japan will be stuck with another environmental hazard to deal with. They cannot be recycled and there is no safe place to deposit them permanently.

- □ 緯度　latitude
- □ 蓄電する　store electricity
- □ 遊休農地　disused field
- □ 山肌　mountain slope
- □ ～に依存する　depend on
- □ 決して環境に優しいとはいえない　not particularly environmentally friendly
- □ 素材　material
- □ 経年劣化　time-related deterioration
- □ 環境問題　environmental problem
- □ ～を抱える　burdened with
- □ 恒久的に　permanently

Plastic

For decades, foreign residents and visitors in Japan have remarked on the excessive wrapping of gifts by department stores. It seemed that there were several layers of cardboard, paper, and plastic around every purchase, and most of it would end up being trashed or recycled. Fortunately, those days are gone and stores are reducing the amount of wrapping that they use. This is particularly true of the plastic that is used.

- □ 見受けられる　be seen
- □ 過剰包装　excessive wrapping
- □ 言及する　mention
- □ 購入品　purchased goods
- □ 段ボール　cardboard
- □ 何重にも　in layers
- □ 廃棄される　trashed
- □ 簡素化　simplification

　しかし、日本(にほん)のペットボトルにはまだ問題(もんだい)が多(おお)い。日本各地(にほんかくち)の電車(でんしゃ)の駅(えき)やオフィスビル、さらには路上(ろじょう)に置(お)かれた自動販売機(じどうはんばいき)はペットボトルに入(はい)った飲(の)み物(もの)を何百種(なんびゃくしゅ)と排出(はいしゅつ)する。意識(いしき)の高(たか)い消費者(しょうひしゃ)なら空(から)のペットボトルをごみ箱(ばこ)や道端(みちばた)に放置(ほうち)せず、きちんとリサイクル用回収箱(ようかいしゅうばこ)に入(い)れるだろう。しかし、日本(にほん)ではリサイクルが間(ま)に合(あ)わず、何(なん)トンもの圧縮(あっしゅく)されたペットボトルが倉庫(そうこ)に蓄積(ちくせき)している。

　進展(しんてん)が見(み)えてきたものもある。コンビニやスーパーマーケットでレジ袋(ぶくろ)が有料(ゆうりょう)になり、エコバッグの携帯(けいたい)が促(うなが)された。レジ袋(ぶくろ)を購入(こうにゅう)する場合(ばあい)でも数円程度(すうえんていど)だが、少(すく)なくとも今(いま)まで当(あ)たり前(まえ)だったものに対(たい)して、今(いま)や購入代金(こうにゅうだいきん)に袋代(ふくろだい)が含(ふく)まれていないことを消費者(しょうひしゃ)は意識(いしき)させられるようになった。中(なか)には数円(すうえん)を払(はら)わないで済(す)むように「マイバッグ」を持(も)ち歩(ある)く者(もの)も増(ふ)え、使(つか)い捨(す)て袋(ぶくろ)の利用(りよう)が減(へ)った。レジ袋(ぶくろ)の有料化(ゆうりょうか)は、消費者(しょうひしゃ)に多少(たしょう)なりとも影響(えいきょう)があった。

　また、コロナ禍(か)で新(あら)たな問題(もんだい)が生(しょう)じた。客(きゃく)の入店数(にゅうてんすう)を制限(せいげん)され休業(きゅうぎょう)を迫(せま)られた飲食店(いんしょくてん)は、テイクアウトのメニューを開発(かいはつ)した。中(なか)には自分(じぶん)のエコバッグを持(も)ってくる客(きゃく)もいるが、食(た)べ物(もの)を持(も)ち帰(かえ)るすべを持(も)たずに購入(こうにゅう)する客(きゃく)もいた。さらに大(おお)きな問題(もんだい)は、食品(しょくひん)を入(い)れるプラスチックや発泡(はっぽう)スチロールの容器(ようき)だ。多(おお)くのテイクアウト用食品(ようしょくひん)が液体(えきたい)や油(あぶら)を含(ふく)むので、漏(も)れないようにしなければならなかった。この問題(もんだい)に対処(たいしょ)するために、一部(いちぶ)では紙製(かみせい)の容器(ようき)を上手(じょうず)に利用(りよう)したところもある。コロナ禍(か)によるプレッシャーが、主要(しゅよう)な環境問題(かんきょうもんだい)を解決(かいけつ)するのに間接的(かんせつてき)に貢献(こうけん)した形(かたち)だ。

But plastic bottles, known as PET bottles in Japan, are still an issue. Vending machines in train stations and office buildings and on streets throughout the country dispense hundreds of types of drinks in plastic bottles. Conscientious consumers place their empty bottles in recycling bins rather than tossing them in the trash or on the roadside. But tons of crushed empty bottles accumulate in storage because the recycling process in Japan cannot process them fast enough.

Significant progress has been made, however, through the encouragement of carrying eco-bags and the introduction of a small fee for plastic bags at convenience stores and groceries. Although customers pay only a few yen to receive a plastic bag for their purchases, they are made conscious of something that they used to take for granted: bags aren't included in the price of the items purchased. Some have developed the habit of carrying a *maibaggu* to the store to save a few yen, and to reduce the need for one-use plastic. The small charge for a plastic bag has had some impact on customers.

As a result of the pandemic, another challenge arose. Facing either restricting customer numbers or shutting down completely, many restaurants developed take-out meals. Some customers brought their own eco-bags, but others arrived to make purchases without the means of carrying them away. The bigger challenge has been to replace plastic and Styrofoam containers for the food itself. Given that a significant portion of take-out food has liquid or oil, it is essential to prevent it from leaking. Innovative uses of paper came into at least partial use in solving this issue. The pressure resulting from the pandemic has indirectly contributed to solving a major environmental problem.

□意識の高い　conscientious
□圧縮された　compressed
□蓄積する　accumulate
□進展　progress
□携帯(すること)　carrying on
□意識させられる　made conscious of
□使い捨て　disposable
□すべ　way, method
□発泡スチロール　Styrofoam
□問題に対処する　addressing the problem
□間接的に　indirectly

防災

ぼうさい

Disaster Prevention

27

防災
災_{さい}

Disaster Prevention

❑ 南海トラフ地震への備え

　2011年3月11日の東日本大震災と津波は、日本の他の場所もいつ洪水や津波のような災害に襲われるかわからないことを実感させた。中でも東京から西に向かって九州まで伸びる沿岸一帯が注目されている。

　日本の太平洋側南西の沖に伸びる南海トラフとして知られる場所で大地震が発生したら、巨大な津波が発生すると言われている。また今後30年以内に70％の確率で大地震が起こるであろうと予測されている。それがいつのタイミングになるのかは予測できないが、その可能性は深刻に受け止められなければならない。

　静岡県から九州にかけての沿岸地域に住む人々は心配であろうが、災害を防ぐために取られてきた施策はそう多くない。危険度が高いと言われる場所に新たな住宅や公共施設を建てないようにしているが、既存の施設や住宅をより高台に移転させることなどは行われていない。ほとんどの住民にとって高台への移転は、その多くが高齢であることもあり、たとえ国が移転費用を一部負担したとしても難しい。

Preparations for a Nankai Trough Earthquake

The Great East Japan Earthquake and the tsunami which followed it on March 11, 2011, brought attention to other areas of the country that are susceptible to flooding, tsunami, and other disasters. One area in particular is along the coast westward from Tokyo as far as Kyushu.

Areas along the central to southwest Pacific coast of Japan are forecast to be hit by an enormous tsunami if a massive quake occurs along what is known as the Nankai Trough, a shallow trench off the coast. Predictions range above 70% that a major quake will occur there within the next 30 years. While there is no way to predict the timing of such an event, the possibility is being taken seriously.

People who live in the coastal areas from Shizuoka to Kyushu have good cause to be concerned, but little has been done to pre-empt a disaster. What has been done is to avoid new construction of homes and public facilities in the areas designated as being at risk of disaster. But little has been done in terms of relocating current structures and homes to higher ground. For most local residents, many of whom are older, even with a relocation subsidy from the government, moving to higher ground would be difficult.

□洪水　flooding

□災害　disaster

□沿岸一帯　all along the coast

□沿岸地域　coastal area

□施策　measure

□高台　higher ground

□移転する　relocate

28

❏ 規制が守られない

防災

Disaster Prevention

　2021年7月の集中豪雨の際、静岡県熱海市の住宅地で大規模な土石流が発生し、土砂が民家を押し流して数キロ先の海まで流れていった。似たような災害は九州や四国で毎年のように起こるが、今回の災害は際立っていた。

　初期対応として生存者と行方不明者の確認が行われ、その後、被害に遭った場所では重機が使用できなかったため、手作業で土砂が取り除かれた。

　その間、専門家は、過去に土砂災害に見舞われたことのない地域でなぜ土砂崩れが起こったのか、原因を探った。そこで明るみに出たのが、新たな形の国の無作為と不法投棄であった。ある会社が建設現場から出た残土を熱海の山に処分するための許可を申請した。

　地元自治体は、降雨などによって水がたまって土が崩れないよう排水設備を事業者が設置することを条件に、盛り土の建設を許可した。この時点まで全て規制に沿って事が進んでいた。地元自治体からすれば、規制があり、それが守られていれば問題はないというわけだ。

　だが、投棄を行った会社は、申請した1.5万立方メートルではなく5万立方メートルもの残土を無断で持ち込んだ。しかもその残土には、許可されていない産業廃棄物も含まれていた。行政は数年にわたり事業者に対して、規則に反しているとの「指導」を繰り返した。

　しかし、何も対策は取られなかった。行政は事業者を罰することもせず、盛り土が崩れて住宅地の細い道を流れ落ちないよう、フェンスなどを建設する命令を出すこともなかった。規制はなんの意味も持たなかった。実施されていなかったからだ。

　豪雨が襲った時、盛り土は崩れ、下の住宅地を目掛けて家を流し、住民を生き埋めにし、熱海市の一角を太い泥の帯で覆った。

Regulations Unenforced

During the torrential rains of July 2021, an enormous mudslide poured through a residential area in Atami, Shizuoka Prefecture, wiping houses away and carrying debris several kilometers to the ocean. Similar disasters strike Kyushu and Shikoku almost every year, but this event stood out.

The first response was to attempt to locate survivors and determine who was still missing. This was followed by the arduous task of removing mud by hand from the devastated area, because heavy equipment could not be used.

Meanwhile experts were tasked with trying to discover how such an event could have occurred in an area with no previous serious mudslides. What came to light is another form of lack of government action and illegal dumping. A company that brought soil from some construction site applied for a license to deposit it in the mountains above Atami.

Apparently the deposit, which was supposed to be pure soil, was allowed by the local government with the condition that drainage pipes would be installed to prevent water from accumulating and making the deposit unstable. To this point, everything went according to regulations. From the perspective of the local government, if there is a regulation and it is met, then everything is fine.

But the dumping company brought not just the registered 15,000 cubic meters of dirt but 50,000 cubic meters, without notifying the government. Included in that soil was industrial waste, which should not have been allowed. Over the years, the government gave repeated "guidance" to the company regarding its violations of the regulations.

However, nothing was done. The government did not penalize the company or force it to construct barriers to prevent the dumped material from sliding downhill, right into a narrow funnel of residences. The regulations meant nothing because they were not enforced.

When the heavy rains came, the whole deposit broke loose and at high speed ripped through the area below, wiping away home, burying residents, and covering a broad strip of Atami in mud.

□集中豪雨　torrential rain
□土石流　mudslide
□土砂　sediment
□際立つ　stand out
□初期対応　first response
□生存者　survivor
□重機　heavy equipment
□明るみに出る　come to light
□無作為　inaction
□不法投棄　illegal dumping
□残土　surplus soil
□処分する　dump
□盛り土　fill
□規制　regulation
□投棄　dumping
□立法メートル　cubic meter
□無断で　without permission
□産業廃棄物　industrial waste
□行政　government
□事業者　business operator
□指導　guidance
□実施する　enforce
□〜を目掛けて　aim at
□泥　mud

29

❏ リスクマネジメント

防災

Disaster Prevention

　日本もかつては世界で最も進んだ国と称され、経済力があり、電子機器の発明に長け、伝統文化とアニメやマンガの想像力が融合するなど羨望のまなざしで見つめられた国であった。

　しかし21世紀に入って20年が過ぎ、その評判は**リスク管理の欠如**により**汚されている**。この類いの議論で頻繁に現れる言葉が、全く期待していなかった、想像をしていなかった、という意味の「**想定外**」だ。この言葉が乱用されるということは、危機的状況で**責任当局**がそのようなことが起こる可能性を全く考慮していなかったことを示唆する。彼らは、そのような**不測の事態**に備える必要はないと当然のように思っている。

　明らかな対策不足の兆しが見えたのは福島原発のメルトダウン事故だ。誰も津波が原発の電力を失わせる可能性があるとは考えず、全ての**非常用電源**を**無用の機器**にしてしまった。この失敗は「**原発の安全神話**」を信じる気持ちと、**最悪の事態**を想定し、その対策を講じるという想像力の欠如に起因する。

　原子力発電を**推進する者**たちは、規則が整っており、規則を守ってさえいれば問題はないという**希望的観測**に陥っていた。このような保証を信じた者たちは、発電に用いた燃料以上に燃料を生み出すとうたわれ、1000億ドル（約11兆4000億円）かけて建設された**高速増殖原子炉**「もんじゅ」が問題を起こし続けていることを無視しているようだ。1995年に発電を開始して以来、電力はたった1時間しか生み出されていない。その1時間に続いたのは複数の事故だ。しかし、政府は議論を**先送り**しては、お金を使い続ける。下手な**比喩**を用いるならば、経済的ブラックホールだ。国が廃炉を決めたとしても、生み出した燃料を吸収できる原発は他にない。

Risk Management

Japan was once considered one of the most highly advanced countries in the world, powerful in economic terms, stunning in electronic inventiveness, and admirable for its combination of traditional culture and popular animation and manga creativity.

But in the third decade of the twenty-first century, its reputation is tarnished by a lack of risk governance. One term that has repeatedly appeared in discussions of this fault is *soteigai*, meaning beyond expectation, completely unimagined. The frequent use of the term has suggested that the responsible authorities in critical situations never considered the possibility that such an event might occur. They assumed that they did not have to prepare for such contingencies.

The obvious early sign of this lack of preparedness was the Fukushima No. 1 nuclear power plant meltdown. No one had considered the possibility that a tsunami would lead to a blackout in the power plant, turning all emergency power generators into useless equipment. Critics attributed this failure to the belief in the "myth of safety of nuclear plants" and a total inability to imagine—much less prepare for—a worst-case scenario.

The promoters of nuclear energy had fallen into wishful thinking that regulations were in place and there would be no problems if the regulations were followed. These believers in guarantees seemed to ignore the continuing problems with *Monju*, a fast-breeder reactor that is supposed to generate more fuel than it consumes, cost $10 billion to build. It has generated electricity for only one hour since it was inaugurated in 1995. That single hour was followed by a series of accidents. And yet the government has to spend money just to mothball it. It is, in an awkward metaphor, an economic black hole. Even if the government decommissions it, there are no other nuclear-power plants that can consume the fuel it has already produced.

□〜に長ける　be skilled at
□羨望のまなざし　look of envy
□リスク管理　risk governance
□〜の欠如　lack of
□汚される　tarnished
□この類いの　this kind of
□想定外　beyond expectations
□乱用する　abuse
□責任当局　responsible authorities
□不測の事態　contingency
□非常用電源　emergency power generator
□無用の　useless
□機器　equipment
□原発の安全神話　myth of safety of nuclear plants
□最悪の事態　worst-case scenario
□推進する者　promoter
□希望的観測　wishful thinking
□〜に陥る　fall into
□うたう　claim
□高速増殖原子炉　fast-breeder reactor
□先送りする　mothball
□比喩　metaphor

使用済みの核燃料棒をどうするかも考えられていない。日本は地震大国でありながら、そのような危険な物質を安全に貯蔵できるところはない。東京電力、関西電力、原子力規制委員会はその小さな問題を見逃しているようだ。地方自治体も同じで、原発が雇用を生み、問題を抱える地元に国が潤沢な補助金を与え続けることを期待する。

　準備不足と、なんとかなるだろうという楽観的な姿勢が顕著に出たのが、日本の新型コロナウイルス対策だ。2020年2月にダイヤモンド・プリンセス号が横浜港に入港した時にはPCR（ポリメラーゼ連鎖反応）検査の数が不足していた。2009年のH1N1亜型インフルエンザの流行時に政府が招集した専門家諮問委員会は、保健所機能の強化、PCR検査の拡充、非常用設備の備蓄や国産のワクチン開発などを提言した。しかし、流行が収まると、国は手綱を緩めた。そして新型コロナウイルスが現れた時、日本の準備不足が再び露呈した。

高速増殖原子炉「もんじゅ」
Monju a fast-breeder reactor

No thought at all is given to where spent nuclear fuel rods will end up. Japan is one large volcanic zone, and there is no place to safely deposit such dangerous materials. Yet the government, TEPCO, KEPCO, and the Nuclear Regulatory Authority (NRA) seem to overlook that minor issue. And local governments do the same, counting on such facilities for jobs and hoping the government will continue generous subsidies to support their troubled communities.

The major instance of lack of preparation and a casual assumption that everything will be all right is Japan's response to the COVID-19 epidemic. The Diamond Princess entered Yokohama harbor in February 2020 and there were an insufficient number of polymerase chain reaction (PCR) tests available. Following an outbreak of A/H1N1 influenza in 2009, a panel of experts appointed by the government submitted proposals for strengthening public health centers, boosting PCR testing capabilities, stocking emergency supplies, and promoting domestic development of vaccine. But once that pandemic was contained, the government relaxed its governance. When COVID arrived, the lack of preparedness became obvious again.

☐使用済みの核燃料棒　spent nuclear fuel rod

☐貯蔵する　store

☐原子力規制委員会　the Nuclear Regulatory Authority

☐潤沢な　generous

☐楽観的な姿勢　optimistic attitude

☐顕著に　remarkably

☐亜型　subtype

☐専門家諮問委員会　panel of experts

☐保健所　public health center

☐拡充　boosting

☐備蓄　stock

☐手綱を緩める　slack the reins

☐露呈する　expose

教育

Education

❏ 学校教育の諸問題——ひとクラスの生徒数

教育
Education

30

　日本の学校教員は働き過ぎだ。**教務や部活の監督**に加えて、**事務作業で忙殺される**。彼らは**放課後も残業し**、多くの場合、その分は**無報酬**である。つい最近まで、**給食費を徴収する**ために夜間、場合によっては週末に、**滞納している親**のところを訪問しなければならず、さらに残業時間が増えていた。

　中には**体調を崩して休職する教員**もいた。とある報告書によると、2019年には5,478人の教員が一般的な病ではなく、**うつ病で休職**したそうだ。

　さらに教職への就職を左右する要素がある。大多数の教師は仕事に対しても学生に対しても大変熱心である。過去には、教師というと、教育への貢献や**献身**が大変尊敬され、優秀な大学を卒業した学生が、こぞって教職を目指した。しかし、その時代はすでに終わったようだ。他の仕事の方が給料も高いし、**労働環境**も良い。また教師が直面するストレスも**周知のこと**だ。

　その要因の一つに、ひとクラスの生徒数の多さがある。2020年まで、小学1年生の生徒数は最大35人とされていた。2年生から6年生までの最大数は40人。生徒が多ければ多いほど、責任も重くなる。また、小学5年生と6年生に英語が**必須科目**として導入されたことで、多くの教師が**苦手と感じる科目**を教えなければならならないというプレッシャーが加わった。

Education Issues: Class Sizes

Japan's school teachers are overworked. In addition to classroom duties and club oversight, they are burdened with administrative tasks. Many have to stay after school and put in overtime which is often unpaid. Tasked with collecting school lunch money from parents, until recently teachers had to call on the homes of parents who were delinquent in paying, in the evenings or on the weekends, adding to their overtime hours.

Some teachers have ended up taking sick leave. According to one report, in 2019 some 5,478 teachers took time off to deal not with ordinary illness but with depression.

There is another element that affects teacher recruitment. The majority of teachers are highly devoted to their work and to their students. In previous periods, teachers were greatly respected for their contributions and their devotions to education, so well-qualified college graduates competed in large numbers to take teaching positions. But those days seem to be over. Other types of work pay better and offer better employment conditions. And the stress that teachers endure is well publicized.

One factor in this is the large number of students in each class. Until 2020, the maximum size of first-year elementary school classes was 35. For second-grade through sixth-grade it was 40. The more students there are, the heavier the responsibilities become. With the introduction of English as part of the curriculum in fifth- and sixth-grade classes, there is the added pressure of having to teach a subject that many teachers are not comfortable with.

- ☐ 教務　classroom duty
- ☐ 部活の監督　club oversight
- ☐ 事務作業　administrative task
- ☐ 忙殺される　be worked to death
- ☐ 放課後　after school
- ☐ 無報酬　unpaid
- ☐ 給食費　school lunch money
- ☐ 徴収する　collect
- ☐ 滞納している　delinquent in paying
- ☐ 体調を崩して休職する　taking sick leave
- ☐ うつ病　depression
- ☐ 献身　devotion
- ☐ こぞって　all together
- ☐ 労働環境　work environment
- ☐ 周知のこと　well publicized
- ☐ 必須科目　required subject
- ☐ 苦手と感じる　not comfortable with

　学校での**各学年**のクラス数は、運によるところが大きい。小学校の6年生を例に取ろう。ある年度の生徒数が70人であれば、上限35人のクラスが2つとなる。それが71人であれば、クラスは3つに分けられ、ひとクラスは23人か24人になる。このような10人少ないクラスであれば、当然教師も個々の生徒との**交流**が増える。採点する答案の数も、生徒の問題対応も、心配する親の対応も若干減る。全てはその年度に入ってくる生徒数で決まる。

　未来も決して明るいものではない。2021年から2025年まで、小学校の各学年の最大生徒数は35人、中学校では40人と定められている。

The number of classes per grade at each school is a matter left to chance. Take for example the sixth grade of an elementary school. If there are 70 students enrolled for that academic year, it means that there will be two full classes of 35 each. However, if there are 71 students enrolled, it means that they will be divided into three classes, with only 23 or 24 students each. These smaller classes, 10 fewer students per class, will allow more interaction between the teacher and the individual students. It will also slightly lessen pressure on the teacher who has to grade fewer papers, deal with fewer student problems, and handle fewer parent concerns. This all depends on how many students enroll in that particular year.

The future is not a whole lot brighter. From 2021 through 2025, the maximum class size of each year of elementary school is set at 35 students. In junior high school classes, that figure is set at 40 students.

□各学年の　per grade
□交流　interaction

31

❑ 学校でのいじめ

日本社会は調和を求め、**目立つことを嫌う**。学校の規則であれ、クラス内の生徒間に存在する**暗黙のルール**であれ、そのルールに従わない個人はクラスの他の生徒に**疎んじられる**ことが多い。教師は事態が深刻になる前にいじめを発見して対処する能力に欠けている。いくつかの**事例**では、教師自身が生徒のいじめに**加担**していた。

地震に津波、さらには原発事故を伴った東日本大震災以降、福島第一原発近くに住んでいた人々は避難を余儀なくされた。多くは遠くの地に定住することを選んだ。その新しい土地でつらい目に遭わされたのが、新しい学校に通うことになった子供たちだ。彼らを歓迎する学校や同級生もいたが、**メディアを賑わした**のは、**顕著**ないじめの事例だ。

福島県から横浜市に移ってきた**被災者一家**の男の子は、新しいクラスメートから**無慈悲**ないじめを受けた。子供たちは彼の**持ち物**を盗み、「バイ菌」呼ばわりした。クラスメートから蹴られ、殴られ、しまいには金を要求した者もいた。いじめに耐えられなくなった男の子は学校を辞めた。

世界のいじめの専門家によると、2～3人の生徒が1人の生徒をいじめるという一般的な**構図**と異なり、日本の学校で起こるいじめには1人の**被害者**をクラスの**大半**がいじめるケースが多い。少数の生徒ではなく、集団の**現象**だ。積極的に参加しない者も、自らへの**報復**を恐れてか、いじめを止めることはしない。その上、いじめた者たちが罰せられることは、ほとんどないのだ。何もせず**傍観者**となった者の中には**悔恨の念を抱く**者もいるだろうが、それより自分が**標的**にならなかったことに安堵するようである。

Bullying in Schools

Japanese society is known for its emphasis on harmony and a desire to avoid standing out. Individuals who don't adhere to the rules—school rules or rules informally agreed upon by the students in a class—are often shunned by other members of the class. Teachers are not known for having the ability to spot bullying or deal with it before it becomes too serious. In several recent cases, teachers have even taken part in bullying individual students.

Following the Great East Japan Disaster, which resulted from an earthquake, a tsunami, and a nuclear plant disaster, families who had resided hear the Fukushima No. 1 nuclear power plant were forced to evacuate. Many eventually relocated permanently in distant cities. Among those who suffered in these new locations were children who had to enroll in new schools. Some schools and classmates were welcoming, but reports of significant bullying have spread across the media.

One boy whose family evacuated from Fukushima to Yokohama was pitilessly bullied by his new classmates. They stole his belongings. They called him "germ boy." He was kicked and beaten by classmates, who eventually began extorting money from him. Unable to stand any further bullying, the boy dropped out of school.

According to experts on bullying across the globe, unlike bullying elsewhere in which two or three students pick on another student, bullying in Japanese schools tends to involve a large portion of a class tormenting one single victim. It is not just a few students, but a group phenomenon. Those who do not actively bully the target do not attempt to stop the treatment, perhaps because they fear being targeted themselves. On top of this, bullies are rarely punished. Those who stand by and do nothing may feel remorse, but they seem to feel relief that they were not the ones who were picked on.

□目立つ　standing out
□暗黙のルール　implicit rule
□疎んじられる　shunned
□事例　case
□加担する　take part in
□定住する　settle
□メディアを賑わした　create a media sensation
□顕著な　significant
□被災者　victim (of some disaster)
□無慈悲な　pitiless
□持ち物　belongings
□バイ菌　germ
□構図　composition
□被害者　victim
□〜の大半　a large portion of
□現象　phenomenon
□報復　retaliation
□傍観者　bystander
□悔恨の念を抱く　feel remorse
□標的になる　be targeted

　いじめの標的になりがちなのは、**同性愛者やミックスルーツの子、またなん**らかの**理由**で自分たちと違うと思われた者たちである。福島県の**惨状**から逃れてきた子供たちは、家が破壊され、また政府によって居住不可と言われるなど、すでにつらい思いをしてきている。彼らは家を失い、学校や多くの友人を失い、中には親戚を失った者もいる。彼らをいじめの標的にするのは**ことさら残酷**である。

Among the common targets of bullying are gay students, children of mixed ancestry, and anyone who is perceived to be in any way different. Evacuees from the Fukushima disaster area are already traumatized by having their homes either destroyed or ruled uninhabitable by the government. They have lost their homes, their schools, many of their friends, and in some cases relatives. Targeting them is especially cruel.

□同性愛者　gay

□ミックスルーツ　mixed roots

□なんらかの理由で　for whatever reason

□惨状　disastrous scene

□ことさら　especially

□残酷　cruel

32

❑ 英語は不可欠か

教育

Education

政府は全ての日本人にとって英語は必須の能力であり、中学校・高校のみならず小学校でも履修科目とするべきだと言う。政治家、官僚、一部の教育専門家は、子供は英語の勉強を始めるのが早ければ早いほど英語を習得しやすいと言う。

英語でコミュニケーションを取れる能力が必要不可欠であることは、当たり前と思われている。しかし、全ての生徒にとって本当に必要なのだろうか。また全ての教員に外国語を教える能力があるのだろうか。

ほとんどの就労者にとって、英語を職場で使うことはまれである可能性がある。業務上の交渉や契約書の作成などは専門家の特殊な技術が必要で、通常の日常会話ができる程度では無理だ。日常会話以上の英語力が必要とされる人材は、企業で働く社員の4分の1未満ではないかと推測される。

サービス業以外に従事する人は、訪日する外国人と必ずしもコミュニケーションを取らなくてもいい。自動翻訳アプリが実際の人対人の英語力に取って代わるなどとだまされてはいけない。これら自動化されたプログラムの多くは非常に劣悪な、時には滑稽な翻訳を生み出す。例えば、大阪メトロは自動翻訳プログラムを使い「動物園前」駅を "Before the Zoo"（動物園の前）、「堺筋線」を "Sakai Muscle Line"（堺筋肉線）と訳した。中でも傑作だったのが「3両目」を "Car Near Eyes 3"（目3近くの車）と訳した。自動翻訳にはまだまだ改善の余地がある。

English as Essential?

The national government has determined that English is an essential ability for all Japanese and should be included not only in junior high and high school curricula, but also in the elementary school years. Politicians, bureaucrats, and some educators contend that children will learn English better and faster the earlier they start.

It is taken for granted that the ability to communicate in English is essential. But is it essential for every student? And is the teaching of a foreign language something that every school teacher is capable of?

The use of English in the workplace is potentially minimal for most workers. The serious business of negotiating business deals and writing contracts require excellent specialist skills, not just everyday conversational skills. One would guess that less than a quarter of all company workers would ever need more than those casual conversation skills.

Communicating with foreigners visiting Japan is not essential for people who are not in the service industries. One should not be fooled into thinking that automatic translation apps will replace actual person-to-person English skills. Many of these automatic programs yield extremely poor, occasionally hilarious, translations. The Osaka Metro once used an automated translation program that gave the English for Dobutsuen-mae as "Before the Zoo" and the Sakaisuji Line as "Sakai Muscle Line." The best of the bloopers was Car No. 3 ("sanryome") as "Car Near Eyes 3." Automated translation obviously needs a lot of improvement.

□履修科目　subject to be studied
□当たり前　natural
□就労者　worker
□業務上の　in the course of business
□交渉　negotiation
□サービス業　service industries
□訪日する　visit Japan
□取って代わる　can replace
□劣悪な　poor
□滑稽な　hilarious
□改善の余地　room for improvement

能力の高い通訳者を必要な現場に導入するのは高価である。しかし、現場に第2言語が**流暢な**人物を置く必要は**必ずしもない**。例えばホテルにチェックインして、出発前に荷物を空港に送るなど、**単純なやり取り**なら電話で通訳してくれるサービスも今は存在する。**やり取りする**2人がそれぞれの言語でしゃべると、通訳者が実際に**現場に**いなくても、話したことを通訳してくれて、やり取りが完了する。

　英語を学び、コミュニケーションを取る真の価値は、文化の異なる人々と個人的に対話し、世の中に対する考えをお互いに**分かち合い**、学ぶことにある。全ての人がこのレベルまで上達するわけではなく、誰もがこれほど難しい課題を強いられるべきではない。**別に**この大きな挑戦を選ぶ人の**やる気を削ぐ**つもりはない。ただこの負担を背負わされた多くの人々の**ためになるとは限らない**ことを単に**指摘**しているだけである。

Having a relatively skilled interpreter on the spot whenever you need one is expensive. However, it is not essential to have a fluent second-language speaker on site. Interpreter services are now available by phone for the most common exchanges, such as checking in at a hotel and arranging package shipment to an airport prior to departure. The two individuals use their own language, the interpreter translates, and the transaction is completed, without the interpreter being physically present.

The real value of learning English and communicating results from personal communication with people of another culture, each sharing his or her own view of the world and learning from one another. Not everyone can get to this level and no one should be forced to take on such a difficult task. This is not to discourage those who choose to take on a huge challenge. It is only to point out that it may not benefit a lot of those on whose shoulders that burden is being placed.

□〜が流暢な　fluent
□必ずしもない　not necessarily
□単純なやり取り　simple exchanges
□やり取りする　communicating
□現場にいる　on site
□分かち合う　share
□別に　not really
□やる気を削ぐ　discourage
□ためになるとは限らない　it may not benefit
□指摘する　point out

❏ 高等教育の無償化

教育
Education

33

　元中央教育審議会の会長である山崎正和氏は、2017年に読売新聞社が発行する英字紙 *The Japan News* に寄稿した記事で、日本の若者に向けて高等教育を無償化することに「低い点数」を付けた。高校や大学の無償化を語るいずれの政党も、日本の若者がそこまで熱く教育を求めているかどうかを考慮していない、と彼は論じた。

　山崎氏の主張するとおり、多くの高校生や大学生は学ぶことにさほど積極的ではない。彼らは他の皆が進学するから進学を選ぶ。入試に合格すると、アルバイトに多くの時間を割き、サークルに属して、なんとか卒業できる程度の単位を稼ぐ。大学3年生は、教育を受ける機会を犠牲にしてまで就職活動に明け暮れる。

　私の個人的な経験も同様の結論を導き出す。授業中に起きている学生は机の下でスマホをいじってばかりだ。授業に来るほとんどの学生は宿題もしてこないし、ノートも取らずに、ただ「出席」するだけ。彼らはそれだけでいいと思っている。印象に残っているある学生は、私の授業に来て最前列に座り、机に突っ伏して授業中ずっと寝ていた。授業が終わって学生が全員出て行っても、私は彼を起こさなかった。怒り心頭で何かしてしまいそうだったからだ。

　代わりに日本の若者は、それぞれの大志を育むような刺激を与えられるべきだ、と山崎氏は提案する。一般的な傾向である大学進学を選ぶより、彼らの興味がある第一次産業や伝統技術の場を選ぶことを推奨すべきだと言う。もし彼らが自らの技術を発展させる学びに喜びを感じることができれば、彼らは必要な専門性や仕事に関連する知識と必要な職業倫理を身につけるだろう。これは生涯学習の最高の形である。

Free Higher Education

In 2017 Masakazu Yamazaki, former chair of the Central Council of Education wrote an article in *The Japan News*, an English newspaper published by The Yomiuri Shimbun, in which he gave "low marks" to the idea of providing free higher education to Japanese young people. He pointed out that none of the political parties discussing the idea of making both high school and university education free bothered to consider whether young Japanese have a burning desire for that education.

As he points out, many high school and university students are unenthusiastic about learning. They opt to continue on to higher education because everyone else tends to do that. They pass their entrance exams, spend a lot of time working part-time, join social circles, and somehow earn enough credits to qualify for graduation. In university, in the third year they engage in job-hunting to the exclusion of getting an education.

My personal experience leads me to the same conclusion. Students who remain awake in class are often fiddling with smartphones under their desk. Most of those who come to class have not read the assignment and do not take notes, but they "attend" and they believe that is all that is necessary. One particularly memorable student came into my classroom, sat in the front row, immediately put his head on his desk, and slept through the entire class. I did not wake him up when class was over and all of the other students left. I was so furious, I was afraid I might do something.

Yamazaki proposed instead that young Japanese should be stimulated to develop their individual aspirations. Rather than following the general tendency to go to university, they should be encouraged to go into primary industries that they find interesting and traditional crafts. If they are stimulated to enjoy learning and developing their individual skills, they will continue to learn the necessary expertise and job-related knowledge and work ethics that they need. This is lifelong learning at its best.

□ 中央教育審議会 Central Council of Education
□ 寄稿する contribute
□ 高等教育を無償化する provide free higher education
□ 主張する argue
□ サークル club, circle
□ 単位 credit
□ 就職活動 job-hunting
□ 同様の結論を導き出す draw similar conclusions
□ 印象に残っている memorable
□ 机に突っ伏す put one's head on one's desk
□ 怒り心頭 so furious
□ 大志 aspiration
□ 育む develop
□ 一般的な傾向 general tendency
□ 第一次産業 primary industries
□ 推奨する recommend
□ 専門性 expertise
□ 職業倫理 work ethics
□ 生涯学習 lifelong learning

<ruby>共<rt>とも</rt></ruby>に<ruby>生<rt>い</rt></ruby>きる

Living Together

34

❏ ジェンダーギャップ

　2021年に発表された世界経済フォーラムの「ジェンダーギャップ指数2021」によると、日本は世界156ヵ国中120位だった。先進国の中では最下位だ。女性の政治家数で計算される**政治参画**の男女差についてはさらに低く、147位と先進国として驚くほど低い。

　国際交流基金の調査報告書には、女性の政治参画の**度合い**が低い理由が述べられている。上位5つの理由の中には、**国会活動**と家庭の両立の難しさ、政治は男性のものだという全体的な雰囲気、女性政治家を**後押しする**環境が整わないこと、それに女性政治家に対する差別やハラスメントが挙げられている。最後の理由は新聞や週刊誌などでもよく取り上げられている。

　男女差はいくつかの分野で顕著である。まず政治分野では、2020年6月の時点で**衆議院**における女性議員は全体の9.9%、**参議院**においては20%ほどである。選挙前になると各政党が女性**候補者**を**擁立する**が、気持ちの変化を表しているというよりは、単なるスローガン作りにしか映らない。自民党は、女性候補者の割合を15%にし、党の**要職**にももっと女性を**起用す**べきだ、と提言している。野党も最終目標を50%とし、まずは30%から35%を女性候補者にすると宣言している。

Gender Gap

According to the World Economic Forum's Global Gender Gap Report in 2021, Japan ranked 120 out of 156 countries in gender equality. That leaves Japan in last place among the major advanced economies. In the field of women's political empowerment, measured by the number of female politicians, Japan rates even lower, at 147, quite unexpected for one of the generally advanced countries.

A survey by the Japan Foundation shows why women are not going into politics. The top five factors mentioned in responses to the survey include difficulty in balancing Diet activities and family life, the overall attitude that politics are for men only, the lack of an environment for encouraging female politicians, and discrimination against and harassment of women politicians. The last factor plays out regularly in the newspapers and weeklies.

The gap between men and women is prominent in several places. First, in the political arena, as of June 2020, women accounted for only 9.9% of lawmakers in the House of Representatives, the Lower House of the Diet, and around 20% in the House of Councillors, the Upper House. Political parties compete with each other to promote female candidates before each election, but rather than indicating a real change in attitudes this seems more like sloganeering. The Liberal Democratic Party proposed measures such as requiring that 15% of all the party's candidates be women and giving more top positions to women. Opposition parties have vowed to aim for women to comprise between 30% and 35% as the first step toward an ultimate target of 50%.

□政治参画　participation in politics
□国際交流基金　the Japan Foundation
□度合い　degree
□国会活動　Diet activities
□後押しする　encourage
□衆議院　House of Representatives
□参議院　House of Councillors
□候補者　candidate
□擁立する　put up
□要職　key position
□起用する　appoint

　男女平等への歩みは単に女性国会議員を増やしたり、女性を会社の取締役に起用したりすればいいだけの問題ではない。女性たちに、実際に**決断を下す権限**が与えられるようにすることが重要である。ジェンダーギャップにおけるこの要素は、元総理大臣で、当時の東京オリンピック・パラリンピック組織委員会の会長であった森喜朗氏が、会議に女性が多く参加すると話が長くなり、他の女性も**追随**して会議がダレると発言したことからも明らかである。これを性差別と呼ぼうが、セクハラと呼ぼうが、要は今日までこのような姿勢が存在しているということが重要だ。本件に関して、森氏は**職を辞して**、元オリンピック選手の橋本聖子氏が会長の座に就いた。

　職場では、「マタハラ」の存在が指摘されている。女性が妊娠したり、産休を取ったりすることで、**嫌がらせ**を受けることだ。女性社員が産休を取ることを「**不便**」と捉えることには、いくつもの問題がある。一つは、女性を責任ある立場に昇進させない言い訳となること。さらには、男性に比べて多くの女性をパートや契約社員、アルバイトに甘んじさせてしまうことである。このような**待遇**では、男性の平均賃金の74％しか女性は平均して稼げないのである。

　働く女性は職場を離れれば家事をすることが「当たり前」という考えがまだ**根強い**中、この**観点**からもジェンダーの平等が得られるかどうかは疑問だ。どのような立場にある男性でも、家事、子育て、介護の責任をもっと担うべきである。2017年には全男性の3.1％しか**法で定められた育児休暇**を取得していない。取得すれば女性の子育ての負担を少しは**軽減**することができるのに。若い男性国会議員が育児休暇を取得した時は、あまりの珍しさにニュースになったほどだ。

Progress toward gender equality is not simply a matter of having women in the Diet or in the boardroom. It is a matter of ensuring that they have actual decision-making powers. This aspect of the gender gap was highlighted by the remarks of former Prime Minister Yoshiro Mori, then-head of the Tokyo Olympic and Paralympic organizing committee, who commented that meetings with lots of women participating tended to drag on because women talked too much and once one woman chimed in every other woman wanted to say something. Whether one calls this sexism or sexual harassment, this attitude has continued to the present day. In this immediate incident, Mori was relieved of his position and replaced with a woman, Olympian Seiko Hashimoto.

In the workplace, one finds *matahara*, harassment for becoming pregnant and taking maternity leave. The "inconvenience" of having a female employee go on leave has several impacts. One is that it is used as an excuse to avoid promoting women to higher positions with heavier responsibilities. Another is that it forces more women than men into part-time, contract, or casual work. In these positions, they earn only 74% of the median male wage on average.

Given the assumption that women in the workplace would "naturally" also tend to all of the household duties when not at the workplace, it is doubtful whether equality of the genders will be reached there either. Men in all positions will need to step up and take on part of the responsibilities for housekeeping, childrearing, and caring for elderly family members. As of 2017, however, only 3.1% of men take their statutory year's paternity leave, which would relieve women of at least a portion of the burden of childrearing. When one young male Diet member actually took paternity leave, it was so unusual that it made all of the media.

□決断を下す権限　decision-making powers
□追随する　chime in
□ダレる　drag on
□職を辞する　be relieved of one's position
□マタハラ　maternity harassment
□産休　maternity leave
□嫌がらせ　harassment
□不便　inconvenience
□言い訳　excuse
□待遇　treatment
□家事　household duties
□根強い　deep-seated
□この観点から　from this perspective
□法で定められた　statutory
□育児休暇　paternity leave
□軽減する　relieve

　働きたい親のために保育所や託児所を充実させる、とする政府の施策も遅々として進まない。職場近くに託児所がないと、親は子供を始業前に預けて、夕方、託児所が閉まる前に急いで迎えに行かなければならないという大きなプレッシャーを抱えることになる。共働き夫婦でも十分大変なのに、これがシングルマザーになると重い足かせになる。子供が小学校に上がっても状況は変わらない。学校が終わったら、具合が悪くなったら、一体誰が子供の面倒を見てくれるのか。援助してくれる親戚でもいない限り、働き続けることは容易ではない。

　政府の重要ポストも、20人の閣僚の中で女性は通常2〜3人だ。大企業の中で、CEOや取締役の座につく女性は一人もいないことが多い。女性が所有する企業の数は、日本の場合、なんとも哀れな17％ぽっちだ。

The government is making little progress in ensuring child-care nurseries for all parents who want to work. Without nurseries near workplaces, parents are under great pressure to drop off their young children before work starts and rush to pick them up before the nursery closes. This is hard enough for working couples, but it puts single mothers in a real bind. It continues to be a problem even when children enter school. Who can take care of children after school lets out, or when they fall sick? Without a relative to help out, it is very hard to keep working.

At the top ranks of government, there are usually only two or three women among the 20 Cabinet ministers. In the large Japanese corporations, chances are that there would not be a single woman as the CEO or board chairperson. As to how many businesses are actually owned by women, in Japan that figure is a dismal 17%.

□託児所　daycare

□遅々として進まない　make little progress

□共働き夫婦　working couple

□重い足かせ　a real bind

□閣僚　Cabinet minister

□なんとも哀れな　what a pathetic

35

□ 医大への不正入試

共に生きる

Living Together

　有名校や有名大学への進学は、何年にもわたる猛勉強と大変競争力の高い入試を経て、受験生の将来を決めるあの運命の日に、合格者の名前が張り出されることで初めて達成される。全ての人に対してオープンで公平な試験だからこそ、最高の候補者が入学してくるものと誰しもが思う。しかし、日本ではそれが普遍的真実ではないようだ。

　一流の医科大学である東京医科大学が、2018年に女性受験生の点数を一律減点させた事実を公表したことに、日本中がショックを受けた。この得点操作は2006年から行われていた。その目的は、大学に進学する女性の割合を30％未満にしておくためだ。

　大学側の言い分だと、その理由は、女性の方が長い医学教育課程の間に結婚出産のために辞めていく可能性が高いからだという。それは、将来の医師不足につながってしまうという。その言い訳が意味することは、女性に平等な機会を与えて医学教育を始めても、家庭の理由で辞めてしまうならば、その1人分がもったいないという考え方だ。大学側は、まるで、やっていたことは完全に正当化されるべきことだと言わんばかりだ。

　このような差別があるのは、東京医科大に限ったことではない。他の医大にも大なり小なり同じような理由で、潜在的に存在する。さらに、忠誠心とスタミナ（なぜか男性を連想させる）が尊ばれる銀行や商社、就職斡旋会社でもよくあることだ。長時間拘束されて融通の利かない労働現場は、家庭には優しくない。これ自体問題だ。しかし、女性が医大に入れないように点数を操作するようなスキャンダルは、明白な日本のジェンダー差別の一例である。ジェンダーのみによって生じる差別である。このような組織的差別は、有能な女性の地位に、有能さで劣る男性が就くことを意味する。

Rigging Entrance to Medical School

Entrance to prestigious schools and universities is achieved by years of intense study, highly competitive entrance exams, and the posting of the names of successful candidates on one fateful day that determines the examinees' futures. It is assumed that the best candidates are accepted because the exam is open and fair to all. But that doesn't seem to be a universal truth in Japan.

Tokyo Medical University, a prestigious medical school, shocked the country when it confessed in 2018 that it intentionally marked down the test scores of female applicants. This manipulation of scores had been carried out since 2006. The aim of this rigging was to keep the percentage of women in each entering class below 30%.

University officials contended that this was because women were more likely to drop out to marry and have children during their long period of medical education. This, the officials said, would leave Japan with a shortage of doctors. The implication was that it was a waste of one slot in the entering class if women were given equal opportunities to begin medical education and later dropped out due to family issues. The university seemed to assume that what they had been doing was completely justifiable.

This form of discrimination is not limited to Tokyo Medical University. It is potentially true at other medical schools, for roughly the same reasons. Further, it is common in banks, trading companies, and job-recruiting agencies where loyalty and stamina—somehow associated with males—are prized. Workplaces with long, inflexible working hours are hardly family-friendly. That is an issue in itself. But the scandal of rigging test scores to prevent qualified women from entering medical school is a clear example of gender inequality in Japan. It is discrimination based on gender alone. And it suggests that this systematic discrimination allows less qualified men to take the places of qualified women.

□競争力の高い competitive
□達成される be achieved
□だからこそ precisely because
□誰しも everyone
□普遍的真実 universal truth
□一律に uniformly
□減点 lower the scores
□得点操作 manipulation of scores
□医学教育課程 medical education course
□正当化される justifiable
□大なり小なり greater or lesser extent
□潜在的に potentially
□連想させる associated with
□尊ぶ value
□就職斡旋会社 job-recruiting agency
□長時間拘束されて融通の利かない労働現場 workplace with long, inflexible working hours
□組織的差別 systematic discrimination

36

❏ #MeToo 運動

日本では、伊藤詩織氏が声を上げるまで#MeToo運動はあまり注目されていなかった。ジャーナリストでありドキュメンタリーフィルムの監督である伊藤氏は、2015年に報道記者の山口敬之氏に就職相談をした際夕食に誘われ、レストランで意識をなくし、数時間後に目覚めるとホテルのベッドで山口氏が自分の上に乗っかっていたと主張した。

日本の法律では、**性被害者**は**同意**がなかっただけではなく、暴行や**強要**があったことを**立証**しなければならない。**後者**ができないと、性的暴行を受けたと**論証**することが難しい。伊藤氏の場合、意識がなかったので、合意がなかったと立証するのが難しかった。

伊藤氏は刑事裁判では負けたが、何が起きたか黙することを拒んだ。彼女は主張を公にした。山口氏に対する**民事訴訟**では、2019年に**東京地裁**が330万円の**賠償命令の判決**を下し、この事件は日本における#MeToo運動の象徴的事案とされた。彼女の2017年の著書『Black Box』(英訳版も出版された)の中で、伊藤氏は社会の意識、文化、社会正義の変革を求める。

さらに**広範な問題**として、主に都内でラッシュ時の満員電車内で起こる女性に対する**痴漢行為**が挙げられる。調査によると、半数以上の女性通勤客が痴漢被害を経験したことがあるというが、犯罪を訴えた者はたったの10%である。警察や鉄道会社に痴漢を訴えても、あまりにも**不毛**なため、被害者も訴えることを諦めてしまうという。中には恐怖や**羞恥心**で訴えることをしない被害者もいる。彼女らは自分の名前や住所、写真までもが公になってしまうことを**懸念**する。また単に職場や学校に遅れてしまうことを嫌がる人もいる。

#MeToo

In Japan, the #MeToo movement seemed to have limited impact until Shiori Ito spoke up. The journalist and documentary filmmaker alleged that she had been sexually assaulted in 2015 by journalist Noriyuki Yamaguchi after discussing a job opportunity over dinner and drinks. She claimed that she lost consciousness at the restaurant and awoke hours later in a hotel bed with him on top of her.

According to Japanese law, the victim must not have consented, but must also prove that violence or coercion were involved. Without the latter, it is more difficult to make a case for being assaulted. In Ito's case the fact that she was in an unconscious state made it hard to prove lack of consent.

Ito lost her case in criminal court, but refused to remain silent regarding what had happened. She went public with her claims. In a civil suit against Yamaguchi, the Tokyo District Court in 2019 awarded her ¥3.3 million in damages, making this incident one of the most significant cases of the #MeToo movement in the country. Her 2017 book *Black Box*—now available in English translation—calls for change in social awareness and cultural change and social justice.

An even broader problem is the groping of women in packed rush-hour trains, particularly in metropolitan Tokyo. Surveys suggest that more than half of female commuters have experienced being groped, but only 10% have reported the crime. Reporting groping, or chikan, to the police or railway companies has generally proven so fruitless that victims have given up even reporting the incidents. Some victims hold back due to fear or even embarrassment. They fear that their name and address and perhaps even their photos will be made public. Others simply do not want to be late in arriving at their workplace or school.

□報道記者　journalist
□性被害者　sexual abuse victim
□同意　consent
□強要　coercion
□立証する　prove
□後者　the latter
□論証する　make a case for
□刑事裁判　criminal court
□主張を公にする　go public with one's claim
□民事訴訟　civil suit
□東京地裁　Tokyo District Court
□賠償命令の判決　judgment for damages
□さらに広範な問題　broader problem
□痴漢行為　groping
□通勤客　commuter
□不毛な　fruitless
□羞恥心　embarrassment

変質者を阻止するためにさまざまな対策が取られている。鉄道会社の中には「女性専用車両」をラッシュ時などに**設けている**ところもある。また**現場**を映像で捉えるべく、車両に監視カメラを設置したところもある。新しく開発されたアプリでは、ユーザーが痴漢行為を報告して、**頻発する**ところを特定しようとするものもある。**警視庁**が開発したアプリは、**起動する**と「やめてください」と声で再生され、近くに痴漢がいることを、「助けてください」の言葉と共に、携帯のスクリーンいっぱいに表示する機能がある。

現在まで、同意のない**性暴力**の立証や痴漢行為の証拠を示す**義務**は被害者側にある。法改正を含む性犯罪に対するさらなる**意識変容**が必要である。

Instead, a variety of efforts have been made to stop the perverts. Several train operators have added special cars marked "women only" for use during the rush-hour periods. Others have installed cameras in the ceilings of cars in hopes of catching molesters on film. One new app enables users to report groping and discover where it is common. Another app created by the Tokyo Metropolitan Police when activated screams "Stop it!" and produces a full-screen messaged saying there is a molester nearby and "Please help."

Until now the burden for proving lack of consent in cases of rape and evidence in the case of groping has been on the survivor. It will take further changes in the law and further efforts to raise awareness about sex crimes.

□変質者　pervert

□阻止する　stop

□設けている　provide

□現場　scene

□頻発する　occur frequently

□警視庁　Tokyo Metropolitan Police

□起動する　activate

□性暴力　sexual violence

□義務　liability (of proof)

□意識変容　altered state of consciousness

37

❏ SNSハラスメントとネットいじめ

共に生きる

Living Together

　ソーシャルメディアで個人に対して**攻撃的で名誉を傷つける**メッセージを投稿することは、世界中で深刻な社会問題となっている。日本も例外ではない。何種類かの明確なターゲットが存在する。

　NBAワシントン・ウィザーズ所属のオリンピック選手八村塁氏と、東海大のバスケットボール選手である弟の八村阿蓮氏は、日々ソーシャルメディアで標的にされ、**黒人蔑視的中傷**や「死ね」などの**罵詈雑言**を浴びせられた。ベナン人の父親と日本人の母親の間に生まれた兄弟は日本で育ち、当然日本語を話し、コメントの意味も十分理解している。日本は**人種差別**のない国であると日本人は信じたいだろうが、ソーシャルメディアで見られるメッセージは日本語で書かれてはいても、まるで**白人至上主義**のサイトから**直接転用された**ような内容だ。

　人種だけが理由ではない。単純に有名であるがためにハラスメントの標的にされることもある。プロレスラーの木村花氏は、海外でも人気のリアリティー番組「テラスハウス」に出演していたが、2020年に**ネットいじめ**の対象とされてしまう。「消えろ」とか「死ね」というメッセージに**耐えかねて**、彼女は自殺してしまった。

　2021年の東京オリンピックを控え、長きにわたる**白血病**との闘いに勝利し、オリンピックへの出場権を獲得した日本水泳界のエース池江璃花子選手は、ソーシャルメディアにオリンピック出場を**辞退するべき**だと投稿されたことを発表した。彼女個人を攻撃したのか、新型コロナウイルスの感染が広がる中、東京オリンピック・パラリンピックを開催することに対する発言なのかは定かではない。しかし、**匿名の投稿による個人攻撃**は、**いかなる人に対しても**向けられるべきではない。日本のオリンピック組織委員会はアスリートを悪意あるコメントから守るべくタスクフォースを立ち上げたが、ソーシャルメディアは、いわゆる**表現の自由**を盾に対策には**後ろ向き**だ。

SNS Harassment and Cyber Bullying

Posting of hostile and defamatory messages aimed at individuals on social media has become a serious social issue around the world, and Japan is no exception. There are several distinct types of targets.

Olympian Rui Hachimura of the NBA Washington Wizards and his brother Aren Hachimura, who plays basketball for Tokai University, have been targeted on social media daily with anti-Black slurs and comments that they "should die." The brothers were born to a Beninese father and a Japanese mother, have grown up in Japan, and, naturally, speak Japanese, so they understand the comments all too well. Japanese would like to think that Japan is a racism-free society, but messages on social media although written in Japanese seem like they are taken directly from a white-supremacist website.

Race is not the only issue. Simply being famous can lead to harassment, too. A professional wrestler named Hana Kimura, who was a cast member in an internationally popular reality show titled "Terrace House" became a cyber-bullying target in 2020. After receiving messages saying "disappear" and "die" she committed suicide.

Prior to the Olympics in 2021, the Japanese swimming star Rikako Ikee, who recovered from a long battle with leukemia before qualifying for a spot in the Olympics, announced that she had received social media messages telling her that she should pull out of the Olympics. Whether the messages were specifically aimed at her or at the decision to hold the Olympics and Paralympics despite the surge in COVID cases in the months leading up to the event was hard to determine. But the personal attacks by anonymous message posters is a burden no one should have to suffer from. The Japanese Olympic Committee set up a task force to shield the athletes from potentially hateful comments, but social media do little to stop so-called freedom of expression.

□攻撃的　hostile
□名誉を傷つける　defamatory
□黒人蔑視的中傷　anti-Black slur
□罵詈雑言　abusive language
□ベナン人　Beninese
□人種差別　racism
□白人至上主義　white supremacy
□転用された　repurpose
□ネットいじめ　cyberbullying
□耐えかねる　unable to bear
□白血病　leukemia
□辞退する　pull out
□匿名の　anonymous
□個人攻撃　personal attack
□いかなる人に対しても　to any person
□表現の自由　freedom of expression
□盾に　use as a shield
□後ろ向き　reluctant to

昔からいじめっ子はいた。彼らは学校の教室に、職場に、公共メディアに出没した。しかしソーシャルメディアは、いじめっ子が匿名で個人や組織を攻撃することを可能にした。彼らは**際限なく**、いやらしい、残酷なことを言い続けられる。**彼らを駆り立てるものが何であれ**、他者を攻撃することで**鬱憤を晴ら**すことに喜びを感じ、その責任を取ることも批判にさらされることもない。デジタル時代の新たなメディアプラットフォームの恩恵を社会は受けるが、その**代償**を、この種のいじめやハラスメントをもって特定の個人に払わせることは、あまりにも大きい。

There have always been bullies. And they have shown their faces in the school rooms, the workplaces, and public media. However, social media allows bullies to anonymously target people and organizations. They can say nasty, cruel things without restraint. Whatever their motivations, they must find some kind of pleasure in venting frustration by attacking others, without having to take any responsibility or face any repercussions. The digital age and media platforms can benefit society, but such bullying and harassment are a hard price for some individuals to pay for those benefits.

□際限なく　without restraint; endlessly

□彼らを駆り立てるものが何であれ　Whatever drives them

□鬱憤を晴らす　vent frustration

□代償　compensation

38

❏ ヘイトスピーチ

共に生きる

Living Together

一つの考え方として、市民は公の場で自分の意見を自由に述べる権利を持っている。たとえ他人がそれに賛同してもしなくても、**民主主義**は彼らが自分の意見を述べる権利を守らなければならない。しかし「ヘイトスピーチ」は全く別次元の話である。

「ヘイトスピーチ」を行ったとされる著名人の中にDHC会長の吉田嘉明氏がいる。**右翼的思想**を持つ彼は、韓国人や韓国人を擁護する日本人に対して暴言を吐く。メディアに対して力を持つ大手企業のトップとして、彼の暴言は彼が率いる企業の方針と見なされる可能性もある。DHCのコマーシャルを流す放送局は、CM自体が自社のガイドラインに**抵触**しない限り、この人物の主張を**黙殺**しがちである。

ジャーナリストやメディアはある意味**苦境**に立たされている。公共の場でのヘイトスピーチの類を取り上げれば、**演説者**の思想を擁護していると非難されるかもしれない。しかし、そうした攻撃的演説を無視すれば、そのような思想を**無批判**に許容していると非難されるかもしれない。現在まで、ほとんどのメディアは吉田氏や右翼、**歴史修正主義者**のような、日本が外国の影響下で危険にさらされていると主張する人物を無視してきた。

しかし評論家が指摘するとおり、ビジネス界もメディアも自らの**社会的責任**を考えるべきである。単純に**広告収入**ばかり見ていると、吉田氏のような人物が**偏見**を主張し、他の人も同様なことをすることを結果的に**容認**したことになる。経済力のある人があのような発言をすることを**無視**したり**黙認**したりすると、世間は差別に**無頓着**になってしまう。日本も他国のメディアも、このような問題を取り上げて**多角的**なものの見方を提示し、世間に対してそれが意味することを理解する手助けをしなければならない。ヘイトスピーチは**無視**したらなくなるのか？　否だ。

Hate Speech

From one perspective, citizens have the right to express their opinions freely in public forums. Whether other citizens agree with them or not, a democracy should protect their right to voice their views. But "hate speech" belongs to a different category.

Among the public figures who are accused of "hate speech" is DHC Corporation's CEO Yoshiaki Yoshida, whose right-wing views single out Koreans and Korean-friendly Japanese in his insults. As head of a large company, which is a major media advertiser, his rants can be taken as principles of the corporation that he heads. Broadcasters that carry DHC commercials tend to remain silent about his views, as long as the commercials themselves do not violate their own guidelines.

Journalists and media are in one sense caught in a bind. If they cover the public tirades of hate-speech types, then they can be accused of encouraging those ideas. If they ignore those tirades, however, they can be accused of allowing the ideas to spread unchallenged. To date, most media choose to ignore people like Yoshida, rightists, and historical revisionists who claim that Japan is in danger of foreign influence.

However, as critics point out, the business world and the media must take into consideration their own social responsibility. If they simply focus on income from the ads, they in effect allow people like Yoshida to express their bigotry and make it acceptable to more people. By ignoring or tolerating such speech by people who have economic power, the public becomes insensitive to discrimination. Japanese media—and that of other countries—needs to cover these issues, show multiple perspectives, and help the public understand what it is all about. Ignore hate speech and it will go away? No.

□一つの考え方として From one perspective

□民主主義 democracy

□著名人 public figure

□右翼的思想 right-wing view

□抵触する violate

□黙殺する remain silent

□苦境に立たされている caught in a bind

□演説者 speaker

□無批判に uncritically

□許容する allow

□歴史修正主義者 historical revisionist

□社会的責任 social responsibility

□広告収入 income from the ads

□偏見 bigotry

□容認する accept

□無視する ignore

□黙認する condone

□無頓着 indifferent

□多角的なものの見方 multiple perspectives

　ヘイトスピーチはある意味深刻ないじめであり、特定の民族、人種、宗教の人々に対する差別に結びつく行為だ。単なる**思想信条の自由**、表現の自由の問題ではない。もしもこれがより広く、何度も提示されれば、中にはそれが真実であるはずだと思ってしまう人も出てくるだろう。ドイツでも20世紀前半にそのようなことが起こった。最近のアメリカも、ソーシャルメディアを通して一つのものの見方に**固執する**人々を見るにつけ、そのような方向に向かっているかのように見える。ヘイトスピーチは単なる言葉ではない。**社会行動**に影響を与え、人が他人を見る目を変えてしまうことができる。この問題にしっかりと**対峙し**なければならない。

Hate speech is, in one sense, a serious version of bullying, tied with discrimination against certain ethnic, racial, or religious groups. It is not simply a matter of freedom of opinion and freedom of speech. If it is widely and repeatedly presented, some people will begin to think it must be true. Germany went that way in the first half of the twentieth century. Parts of America seem to be going that way in recent times with people clinging to social media from one point of view only. Hate speech is not just words. It has consequences in social action, and it can change the way people see other people. It should be confronted.

□思想信条の自由　freedom of thought
□〜に固執する　cling to
□社会行動　social action
□対峙する　confront

39

❑ 国立アイヌ民族博物館の意味

共に生きる

Living Together

　ほとんどの日本人にとって、アイヌとは興味深い文化を持った忘れられた北海道の原住民だ。大勢で歌うことを意味する「ウポポイ」と呼ばれる国立アイヌ民族博物館への来訪者は、そこで掲げられる「民族の調和」というメッセージを温かく歓迎してくれるものと感じるだろう。

　しかしアイヌの歴史は、調和とはかけ離れた歴史である。アイヌ民族は何百年もの間、サハリンのクリル諸島と今の北海道に住んでいた。明治維新を経て、日本政府は北海道を自国の領土であると主張し、島を占領するに等しい行為に及んだ。大挙して押し寄せた日本人に明治政府は土地を無料で与え、それが疫病の蔓延と、原住民の強制労働につながった。この行為を「奴隷制度」と呼ぶかどうかについてはいまだに議論されている。少なくとも、明治政府は先住民の権利に全く配慮せず、ただ単に土地を取り上げ、彼らが自分のものと呼べる場所をなくしてしまったと言える。

　1899年の法律でアイヌは同化を強要され、日本名を名乗り、日本語を話すことを命じられた。この北海道旧土人保護法は100年もの間廃止されずにいた。2007年に日本が「先住民の権利に関する国際連合宣言」に署名したことで初めて、残存するアイヌが先住民族であると日本政府に認められた。しかし、これは単に形式的なことだ。

　ウポポイはアイヌの血を引く人々に仕事を与え、アイヌ芸術家に作品を売る場所を提供するかもしれない。しかし、博物館を開くことで、アイヌの人々に対する過去の過ちを謝罪したことにはならない。またアイヌの人々を偏見から守るものでもない。現代でも就職や結婚の際、アイヌの人々は見下され、差別されるのだ。

The Meaning of the National Ainu Museum

To most Japanese, the Ainu are a commonly forgotten indigenous people in Hokkaido whose culture is somewhat interesting. Visitors to the new National Ainu Museum, called Upopoy ("singing together in a large group"), will find its message of "ethnic harmony" warm and welcoming.

The historical background of the Ainu, however, is a less harmonious story. The Ainu lived for centuries in the Kurile Islands, Sakhalin, and what is now Hokkaido. Following the Meiji Restoration, the Japanese government laid claim to Hokkaido as its own territory, in what amounted to colonizing the island. The government handed out land free of charge to Japanese who arrived en masse, spreading diseases and forcing the local population to work. There is debate as to whether the term "slavery" is appropriate in describing this action. At the very least, the Japanese government paid no attention to the rights of the prior residents and simply took the land, leaving them with no place to call their own.

The Ainu were forced to assimilate by law in 1899, to take Japanese names, and to speak Japanese. The assimilation law was not repealed for a century. Only in 2007, when Japan signed the United Nations Declaration on the Rights of Indigenous Peoples (UNDRIP) did the remaining Ainu gain some recognition as an indigenous group. But that was a mere formality.

Upopoy may provide people of Ainu heritage with jobs and give Ainu artists a place to sell their products. However, the opening of the museum does not constitute an apology for past misdeeds against the Ainu. And it does not protect Ainu from being stereotyped. There is still discrimination in the present day in applying for jobs and from families of romantic partners who believe Ainu are of a lower class.

□原住民　indigenous people

□国立アイヌ民族博物館　National Ainu Museum

□明治維新　Meiji Restoration (1868)

□領土　territory

□占領する　occupy

□大挙して　en masse

□疫病の蔓延　spread of diseases

□強制労働　forced labor

□奴隷制度　slavery

□権利に全く配慮せず　pay no attention to the rights

□同化　assimilation

□北海道旧土人保護法　Hokkaido Former Aborigines Protection Act (1899)

□先住民の権利に関する国際連合宣言　United Nations Declaration on the Rights of Indigenous Peoples

□過去の過ち　past misdeeds

中でも対応が求められるつらい出来事は、日本の研究者によって20世紀初めにアイヌの墓から掘り起こされた遺骨がいまだ返還されていないことだ。大学の保管庫に入れたままなのだ。一部は実際の子孫に返却されたが、他はウポポイの施設に合祀され、個人の子孫に戻されていない。そのような無神経さは耐え難い。日本人だって、第二次世界大戦時に海外で戦死した日本人の遺骨を返還させるために多くの努力を払っているではないか。アイヌの文化やアイヌの子孫を大事に思う人々にとって、ウポポイの施設は新たな軽視を示しているに過ぎない。遺骨は「返還」されたが、このような状態に至ったことに対する謝罪は一言もない。

土地を取り上げ、先住民を強制的に同化させる行為は、ヨーロッパの開拓者がアメリカ先住民に行ったことや、イギリスがオーストラリアのアボリジニに行ったこととかなり似ている。土地を取り上げ、特別保留地に強制移住させ、子供たちを遠い学校に追いやって自分たちの文化を蔑むように教育し、自分たちが子供の頃にしゃべっていた言語を話すと罰する。その後、開拓者の子孫が彼らの文化を楽しめる博物館を建てる。このプロセスは不愉快なほど見覚えがある。

アイヌの一家
the Ainu family

One particularly poignant issue remaining to be dealt with is that the majority of remains taken from Ainu graves in the early 20th century by Japanese researchers have not been returned. They are held in university archives. A few of the remains were returned to actual descendants of the deceased. Others that were returned are simply consolidated in a facility at Upopoy, not returned to those individuals' descendants. That lack of sensitivity is hard to endure, especially given the efforts the Japanese themselves have made to return remains of their people from overseas since World War II. To those who hold Ainu culture and their Ainu descendants to be important, the facility inside Upopoy is another sign of disrespect. Yes, the remains are "returned," but there has been no apology for what led to these issues.

The seizure of the land and forced assimilation of its indigenous population is quite similar to what the European colonists did to the Native Americans and what the British did to the Australian Aboriginals. Take their land, force them to move to reservations, send their children to distant schools to be educated to look down on their own culture, and punish them for speaking their childhood language. Then make a museum for descendants of the colonizers to enjoy their culture. The process sounds unpleasantly familiar.

□つらい出来事 poignant issue
□遺骨 remains
□保管庫 archive
□子孫 descendant
□合祀する enshrine together
□無神経さ lack of sensitivity
□新たな軽視 newfound disregard
□特別保留地 reservation
□自分たちの文化を蔑む look down on their own culture
□開拓者 colonizer

40

❑ 移民が求められている

共に生きる

Living Together

　日本はお金を落として経済を支えてくれる観光客には**門戸を開く**。しかし永住するかもしれない移民に対しては、**門戸を閉ざしがちだ**。OECD加盟国では、外国人が国全体の人口に占める割合の平均は12%だが、日本の場合はほんの2%のみだ。

　しかし、日本は**早い時期に労働者が必要**となってくる。**介護施設や保育施設**での人手不足を見れば、日本政府も**生産年齢人口の減少**に対応するために多くの移民の受け入れに**もっと前向きになる**、と人は思うだろう。日本の人口は減少しており、生産年齢人口（15～65歳）は今後数十年にわたり減少が続くと**想定される**。しかし、日本政府は移民を増やすより、少なくとも低賃金なパートや契約社員などとして働く女性が増えたり、全ての日本人がより高齢になるまで働き続けることのほうが好ましいと考えている。

　働き手を増やす**ささやかな手段**として、**未熟練労働者**に対するビザの発行がある。

　国は「**研修生**」という名目で3年程度の期間、外国人が日本で**技術を習得し**、母国に戻ってその技術を広められるようにする制度を設けた。この仕組みであれば来日する外国人は定住者とはならないので、**国にとって都合が良い**。彼らは短期間来日し、労働力を提供し、母国へ帰国する。その代わりに、日本で得た技術をお土産とすることができると政府は主張する。

Immigrants Needed

Japan has generally kept its gates open to tourists who spend money and support the economy. But the country has kept its gates relatively closed when it comes to immigrants who might take up residence permanently. While the average percentage of foreigners in the OECD nations is 12%, foreigners make up only 2% of the population in Japan.

But Japan is going to need workers from somewhere soon. Given the lack of employees in elderly care facilities and childcare nurseries, one would think that the government would be more open to accepting mass immigration to counter the shrinking working-age population. The population of the country is dropping and it is anticipated that the working-age population (ages 15-65) will drop continually for the next decades. The government would be happy to increase the proportion of Japanese women who work—at least in the lower-level, part-time or contract jobs—and keep all Japanese working later in life rather than expanding immigration.

The small steps that have been taken toward meeting this need for workers have focused on visas for low-skilled workers.

The government has made it easier for "trainees," or *kenshusei*, to come to Japan supposedly to gain skills to take back to their home countries after a period of three or more years. This system suits the government because the incoming foreigners will be non-permanent residents. They will come to Japan for a short time, provide labor, and return to their home countries. In return, the government claims, they will take home the skills they have gained in Japan.

□門戸を開く　its gates open

□門戸を閉ざしがちだ　its gates relatively closed

□早い時期に　sooner rather than later

□介護施設　elderly care facility

□保育施設　childcare nursery

□生産年齢人口　working-age population

□減少　decrease

□〜にもっと前向きになる　be more positive toward

□想定される　be anticipated

□ささやかな手段　modest measure

□未熟練労働者　low-skilled worker

□研修生　trainee

□技術を習得する　gain skills

□国にとって都合が良い　convenient for the country

しかし、このビザで来日する人員を単純作業などに従事させるなど、**制度を悪用する企業に対して、国は見て見ぬふりをする**。多くの研修生はほぼ訓練を必要としない仕事に従事させられ、**林業、農業、漁業や食品加工**などのきつい作業を強いられる。研修生と呼ばれる彼らは長時間労働を強要され、休みもほとんど与えられず、病気になり仕事ができなくなると罰せられる。職場以外の日本人との交流はほとんどなく、日本語も日本という国についても学ぶことができない。**結果的に彼らは安い労働力であるだけだ**。母国に持って帰れる技術など取得することは不可能だ。

さらに、この制度を悪用するブローカーの存在がある。彼らは**要するに人身売買を行っている**。東南アジアの国や地域の人々の多くは低賃金で働き、家族を支えるために日本で働いてお金を稼ぎたいがために、借金をして来日する。ブローカーは彼らを日本に誘い、**多様な「援助」で誘惑する**。しかし、この「援助」は**タダではない**。来日して仕事や家を見つけてもらうだけでブローカーから**借金するはめに陥る**。そもそも日本で稼いで家族を支えるために日本に来たのに、彼らはお金を貯めることすらできなくなる。

彼らをそんな**あくどい労働慣行**から守るすべはあまりない。日本政府は研修生の状況を確認して、このようなブローカーや企業に責任を取らせようとはしない。労働者たちには、**通常の状況でも、守ってくれるところがない**。雇い主の中には**最低賃金すら払わない**ところもあるが、このような**不法行為**を止める人もいない。

日本にいる外国人労働者は他国より多くのことで雇用主に頼らなければならない。雇用主の援助なしには携帯電話も入手できないし、**銀行口座も開設**できない。多くの場合、援助なしに住居を見つけることもできない。多くの**家主**は外国人に**物件**を貸すのを嫌がる。貸してくれる家主がいても**保証人**が必要となる。こういったこと全てがブローカーや雇用主に有利に働く。

But the government quickly turns a blind eye to companies that exploit these visa bearers as staff members for low-level jobs. Many of these trainees end up at jobs that involve little or no training and are little more than hard labor in forestry, farming, fishing, or food-processing jobs. The so-called trainees are forced to work long hours, are given little time off, and are punished if they become ill and cannot work. They have little or no contact with the Japanese people outside their workplaces and gain very little knowledge of Japanese language or Japan as a country. In effect, they are simply cheap labor. Most gain no skills that they can take home.

Further abuse of this system comes from the participation of brokers, who are essentially involved in human trafficking. In countries in Southeast Asia and other regions where there are few well-paying jobs, the appeal of working in Japan and making more money to support their families, would-be migrant workers often end up borrowing money to pay their way to Japan. Brokers entice them to come to Japan and tempt them with varieties of "assistance." But this so-called assistance is not free, and the workers end up owing money to the brokers, just to get to Japan and find a job. Then these workers find it hard to save anything to support their families back home, which is the reason they want to come to Japan in the first place.

They have little protection from abusive labor practices. The Japanese government, however, fails to check on the trainees or hold these brokers or the companies accountable. The workers have no one to turn to for protection, even under normal conditions. Some employers do not even pay the minimum wage, and no one stops them from this illegal wage paying.

Foreign workers depend more heavily on their employer than in other countries. Without help, they cannot get a mobile phone or open a bank account. In many cases, they need help getting housing. Many landlords refuse to rent housing to foreigners. The ones who are willing to rent to foreigners require a guarantor. All of this gives control to the broker or the employer.

□制度を悪用する企業　companies abusing the system

□見て見ぬふりをする　turn a blind eye

□林業　forestry

□農業　farming

□漁業　fishing

□食品加工　food-processing

□きつい作業　hard labor

□結果的に　as a result

□要するに　essentially

□人身売買　human trafficking

□多様な　varieties of

□援助　assistance

□タダではない　not free

□借金するはめに陥る　end up owing money

□そもそも　in the first place

□貯める　save

□あくどい労働慣行　abusive labor practices

□通常の状況　normal conditions

□最低賃金　minimum wage

□不法行為　illegal practice

□銀行口座を開設する　open a bank account

□家主　landlord

□物件　property

□保証人　guarantor

さらに状況を悪化させているのが、パンデミックのせいでこのような労働者が仕事を失っていることだ。中には払われるべき給料も支払われず、**会社の寮**を追われ、政府からも何の援助も受けられない者もいる。仕事も住むところもなくし、帰国するための飛行機代もない彼らは**身動きが取れない**。**慈善団体**などの援助すら得られない者は、**非合法な仕事**に就いてしまう。

家族のためにたくさん日本で稼ぎたいと**純粋**に思って来日する移民労働者がいる中、日本政府にはこの**技能研修制度**が悪用されないようにする義務がある。政府はいつまでも「強制労働を排除すべく**鋭意努力している**」などと口先だけの発言を繰り返している場合ではない。国はブローカーや雇い主がきちんと責任を果たし、移民がどのように扱われているかを**注意深く監視**しなければならない。

What's worse is that with the pandemic, many of these workers have lost their jobs. In some reported cases, they were not given wages that were due to be paid, were told to leave company dormitories, and received no assistance at all from the government. With no job, no place to live, and no money to pay for a plane ticket to their home country, they were stuck. Without assistance from charities, some ended up in illegal businesses.

While some migrant workers may come to Japan with naive ideas about earning a lot to send home to their families, the Japanese government has a duty to ensure that the technical intern system is not abused. The government cannot simply continue to offer platitudes about "making concerted efforts to stamp out forced labor." It must actually hold recruiters and employers accountable, and carefully monitor how migrants are treated.

□会社の寮 company dormitory

□身動きが取れない stuck

□慈善団体 charities

□非合法な illegal

□純粋に思って with naive ideas

□技能研修制度 technical intern system

□鋭意努力している making every effort

□口先だけの発言 insincere statement

□注意深く監視する carefully monitor

41

❑ 難民認定

共に生きる

Living Together

日本には推定8万2000人もの外国人が不法滞在しているとされている。彼らは観光ビザや就労ビザで入国し、それぞれのビザが切れてもそのまま滞在を続けている。ある意味、彼らは単純に「消えて」しまっていて、警察や法務省も彼らがどこへ行ってしまったかわからない。自らの生活を支える何らかの仕事を見つけたのであろうと推測されるが、中には非合法な仕事に就いている者もいるだろう。

国は、こういった人々を発見した場合、国外退去を命じる。命令を受けて母国へ戻った外国人は年間1万人にも及ぶが、まだ3,000人ほどが国内にとどまっている。

後者は何度も難民申請を行う。申請手続きが行われている間は自動的に滞在を続けられるからだ。2021年3月、スリランカ出身のウィシュマ・サンダマリ氏が入管施設に収容中に亡くなった時、この難民申請の問題は大きく注目された。彼女は職員に何度も病院での診療の機会を求めたが受け入れられず、最後は33歳で一人、独房の中で亡くなった。

難民申請は日本に滞在する手段程度に捉えられているかもしれない。しかし、申請者の多くは、母国に強制的に送還されると大きな危険にさらされ、命さえも脅かされるのだ。危険の理由は宗教的、政治的信条や人種問題かもしれない。母国が混乱していると、危険はさらに高まる。アフリカのサヘル地域や中東の国々からの難民などにとって、母国に戻って命の危険にさらされることを恐れるのは極めて正当な思いだ。

Refugee Status

It is estimated that some 82,000 foreigners are illegally overstaying in Japan. These foreigners have entered Japan on a tourist visa or a working visa and have stayed beyond the time limit stated on that visa. In a sense, they simply "disappear" and law enforcement agencies do not know where they are. One assumes that they have found some kind of work to support themselves, but also suspects that sometimes they are working at illegal jobs.

If the government locates one of these people, it issues a deportation order. On an annual basis, some 10,000 foreigners return to their countries after receiving these orders, but another 3,000 remain in Japan.

The latter make repeated applications for asylum, because that automatically allows them to stay while their applications are processed. The issue of asylum received serious attention in March 2021 with the death, while being detained by immigration authorities, of Wishima Rathnayake, from Sri Lanka. After her repeated requests for release for medical treatment at a hospital were denied by authorities, she died alone in her cell at the age of 33.

Application for asylum may seem like little more than a strategy for remaining in Japan. However, for a significant portion of these applicants, there is a real danger that if they were forced to return to their home countries, their lives would be endangered. The danger could be due to their religious beliefs, their political views, or ethnic conflict. It is particularly serious when the home country is in turmoil. Refugees from certain countries in the Sahel in Africa and the Middle East are entirely justified in fearing for their lives if they return.

□推定　estimate
□不法滞在　illegal overstaying
□観光ビザ　tourist visa
□就労ビザ　working visa
□法務省　Ministry of Justice
□推測する　assume
□国外退去を命じる　issue a deportation order
□難民申請　application for asylum
□自動的に　automatically
□入管施設　immigration facility
□収容中に　while being detained
□診療　medical treatment
□独房　cell
□日本に滞在する手段　strategy for remaining in Japan
□強制的に送還される　be forced to repatriate
□脅かされる　be endangered
□混乱している　in turmoil

　日本で難民申請をしている者の中に、学生や研修生として正規のビザで来日したミャンマー人がいる。母国を離れている間に政府転覆があり、中には日本で**合法的な抗議運動**に参加し、名前や写真が**公にされている**者もいる。彼らは帰国して**拘束される**ことを恐れる。結果、難民申請するか、単純に「消えて」しまうか以外に手立てがない。

　国連難民高等弁務官事務所（UNHCR）は、日本のこのような対応を**非難**してきた。国連の専門家は日本の現状の政策や**改正案**は**人道的観点**から**国際的基準を満たしていない**と言う。

　現在、日本で難民申請が認められる人は全体の1％だ。2020年には3,936件の申請があり、そのうち47件のみが認められた。国際的基準に照らしても、**あり得ないほど低い**。

　改正案では、申請をする人々が認められることが、さらに難しくなる。なぜならば、難民申請した外国人が3回拒絶されると、強制送還されることもあるからだ。

156

Among those who are currently seeking legal refuge in Japan are citizens of Myanmar who have come to Japan with legitimate visas as students and trainees. Due to the government takeover in their home country during their absence, some have participated in legal protests in Japan and their names and photos are in the public domain. They fear that they will be taken into custody if they return. As a result, they have no alternatives other than to apply for refuge or simply "disappear."

The United Nations High Commissioner for Refugees (UN-HCR) has criticized Japan for its actions toward such refugees. UN experts say Japan's current policies and proposed revisions fail to meet international standards from the standpoint of human rights.

At present, Japan accepts only roughly 1% of the applications it receives. In 2020, the government certified only 47 applications out of 3,936 that were submitted. By international standards, this is outrageously low.

A proposed law would make it even harder for applicants to succeed. A foreigner who has applied for refugee status three times and been denied that status could be deported.

□政府転覆　government takeover

□合法的な抗議運動 legally compliant protest

□公にされている　made public

□拘束される　be taken into custody

□手立てがない　have no alternatives

□非難する　criticize

□改定案　proposed revisions

□人道的観点　standpoint of human rights

□国際的基準を満たしていない　fail to meet international standards

□あり得ないほど unbelievably

生活・文化

せいかつ　ぶんか

Daily Life and Culture

❏ コンビニの最終決戦

生活・文化

Daily Life and Culture

42

　日本はどこにでもコンビニがある。郊外の道路の反対側や、都市部の交差点の対角線上など、互いに見える距離にあったりする。店舗によって置いてある商品も異なるが、文具、着替え用の下着、雑誌、酒、その場で温めてくれる弁当類などがコンビニの魅力の一端だ。

　この日本式のコンビニをさらに便利にするのが、24時間営業だ。早朝から活動する人や夜通し遊ぶ連中、暗闇の中、行き場所を求める不眠症の人などにとって最高の場所である。しかし、ある人々はこの仕組みに苦しめられている。フランチャイズ店のオーナーたちだ。

　日本に5万店舗以上あると言われるコンビニの4割をセブン-イレブンが占めており、彼らの業態が業界のスタンダードとなっている。日本のセブン-イレブンは、直営店とフランチャイズ加盟店より構成されている。持ち株会社であるセブン＆アイ・ホールディングスの本部がルールを作成し、加盟店はそれに従う。言うことを聞かない加盟店など言語道断だ。

　今、問題になっているのが24時間営業という規定だ。加盟店を営むオーナーは通常夫婦で働き、たとえ2人が12時間で交代したとしても、営業を続けるためにはアルバイト従業員を雇う必要がある。時給が低く、夜通しの勤務になるので、長期間働いてくれる信頼できる従業員を見つけるのは至難の業である。中には低い賃金でも働いてくれる、就労ビザを取得した外国人労働者を雇うところもある。いずれにしても、全く休みも取れず、仕事は過酷である。

　24時間営業によって企業は利益が上がるが、労働コストを背負う加盟店のオーナーたちはこの仕組みでは商売が成り立たない。元日のみ休業する、または夜中に数時間休む時短営業をしようとすると、フランチャイズ契約を取り消すと脅されるなど、本部から強い圧力がかかる。

Convenience Store Showdowns

Convenience stores are everywhere in Japan, within sight of one another on opposite sides of suburban roads and on opposite corners of urban streets. What they offer differs from store to store, but stationery, a change of underwear, magazines, alcohol, and ready meals that can be zapped on site are a few of the attractions.

What makes the Japanese version of these stores even more convenient, is that they are open 24 hours a day. This is great for the early risers, the late-night party crowds, and insomniacs looking for some place to go in the darkness of night. But it is hard on one particular group: the franchisees.

Some 40% of Japan's 50,000 plus convenience stores are controlled by 7-Eleven, making it the industry standard for how such businesses are run. Japan's 7-Elevens are operated in two formats, one is directly by Seven & I Holdings, the Japanese holding company, and the other is by franchisees. The holding company headquarters make the rules and the franchisee has to follow those rules. And heaven forbid that a franchisee doesn't obey them.

The current conflict is over the round-the-clock operation requirement. Franchisees are often couples who both work in the store, but even if they each put in 12-hour shifts, they still need part-time employees to carry on their business. Since they offer low pay per hour and need help all night as well, they struggle to find workers who are dependable and stay on long term. Some franchisees employee foreign laborers with work visas, because they are willing to work for lower pay. But the work pace is grueling without a single day off to recuperate.

Corporate profits are lifted by the 24-hour-a-day operations, but the franchisees, who bear the labor costs, regularly find the system unsustainable. If they attempt to shut down for one day at New Year's or for several hours in the middle of the night, the company comes down hard on them, threatening to revoke their franchise contract.

□郊外　suburbs
□対角線上　diagonal
□その場で温めてくれる　be zapped on site
□夜通し　all night
□不眠症の人　insomniac
□フランチャイズ店のオーナー　franchisee
□業態　business conditions
□業界のスタンダード industry standard
□直営店　company-operated store
□フランチャイズ加盟店 franchise store
□構成されている　consist of
□持ち株会社　holding company
□本部　headquarters
□加盟店　affiliated store
□言語道断　outrageous
□規定　regulation
□〜するのは至難の業　be extremely difficult to
□過酷　grueling
□利益　profit
□労働コスト　labor cost
□成り立たない unsustainable
□時短営業　reduced business hours
□契約を取り消す　revoke a contract

2020年9月に公正取引委員会は実態調査を行い、コンビニ業界の24時間営業の方針は立ち行かないとの結論を出した。法令違反の可能性を示唆しつつ加盟店にもっと営業時間に関する裁量権を与えるよう改善を要請した。それに対してセブン-イレブン側は、加盟店の売り上げの取り分を増やし、営業時間に関してより柔軟に対応できるようにした。加盟店側がこれら措置の恩恵にあずかることができるかどうかは今後の課題である。

In September 2020, Japan's Fair Trade Commission concluded in its investigation that the whole convenience store industry's 24-hour-a-day policy is unsustainable. It ordered stores to give franchise owners more flexibility in their operating hours and backed the demand with possible legal action. In response, 7-Eleven did increase its franchisees' share of the revenue from the respective stores and did take a more flexible stance on operating hours. It remains to be seen whether the franchisees will benefit from a degree of flexibility.

□公正取引委員会 Japan's Fair Trade Commission

□実態調査 fact-finding

□方針 policy

□立ち行かない unsustainable

□法令違反 legal violations

□示唆する imply

□もっと裁量権を与える give more discretion

□加盟店の売り上げの取り分 franchisees' share of the revenue

□柔軟に flexible

□〜の恩恵にあずかる benefit from

43

❑ 顧客サービスの低下

生活・文化

Daily Life and Culture

　日本は長い間、サービス産業において従業員が過剰とも言えるほどの気配りと丁寧さで顧客に対応することで知られていた。しかし、時代は変わってきている。そのような従業員の多くはいなくなった。

　誰と入れ替わったかというと、オートメーション化に取って代わられていることが多い。中には入り口を入ると、館内インフォメーションや案内システムによって、探しているサービスを人間と遭遇せずとも見つけることができるようになっている店舗もある。

　「変なホテル」では、ロボットがチェックイン手続きをしてくれる。客によって使う言語が違うので、パネルで自分の言語を選べば、人間と言葉を交わさなくても登録し、支払いし、自分の部屋の鍵を受け取ることができる。

　最近では多少数も減ってきたが、自動販売機は日本への観光客にまず体験してもらいたいものだ。今や自動販売機で、自宅に持ち帰るための冷凍の料理から歯ブラシ、下着などの身の回りの品、アイスクリームやプレッツェル、男性向けスキンケア用品、プラスチックのおもちゃに至るまで購入することができる。中には近づいてくる人をカメラで認識し、AI機能を使って客となりうる人物の性別や年齢を推定し、その人が好みそうなおすすめ商品を提示してくれるものもある。

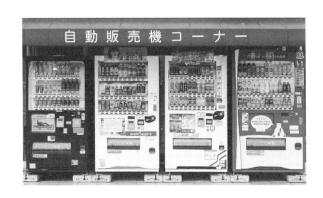

Customer Services on the Decline

Japan has long been known for its service industries where employees pamper customers with almost excessive attention and politeness. But times are changing. Many of those staff members have disappeared.

If they are being replaced at all, it is often by automation. At the entrance to some stores there is an information and guide system that allows you to search the services in the store and find what you want without encountering a human being.

At the Henn na Hotels (literally "strange hotels") the check-in is carried out by robots. Since guests may speak different languages, if you press the panel button for your language, you can complete the entire registration, make the payment, and get a key to your room without exchanging a word with another human being.

Although the number has slightly declined recently, vending machines are still a must-experience when visitors come to Japan. Vending machines can now dispense frozen meals to take home, personal items like toothbrushes and underwear, ice cream and pretzels, men's skin care products, and plastic toys. Some vending machines have cameras facing the customer who approaches it. Using AI recognition functions, it estimates the gender and age of the potential customer and "personally" recommends a product for that person.

□過剰　excessive
□気配り　attention
□丁寧さ　politeness
□入れ替わる　replace
□中には　some (of them)
□人間と遭遇せずとも　without encountering a human being
□変なホテル　Henn na Hotel
□自動販売機　vending machine
□身の回りの品　personal items
□近づいてくる　approach
□認識　recognition
□推定する　estimate
□提示　present

44

❏ データセキュリティ

　スマートフォンのアプリは、多くの日本人にとって非常に魅力的な**利便性を提供する**。中でも主要なコミュニケーションツールとなったのが、LINE アプリだ。すでに国内だけで8,600万人のユーザーを誇る。官庁や地方自治体までもが**行政サービス**を提供するのにLINE を活用してきた。その一例が、2021年の新型コロナワクチンの接種予約だ。

　LINE 株式会社が、中国のソフトウエア企業に**個人情報**へのアクセスを許可していたことは、2021年の3月まで一般の人は知らなかった。個人情報の保護も重要だが、中国により2017年に施行された**国家情報法**や、近年中国人のみならず世界中の個人に対して行われている監視や**偵察行為**に鑑みると、日本政府までもが国家安全保障の観点からLINE アプリのデータを利用するかもしれないと懸念を抱くのも自然なことであろう。

　個人データが利用される可能性は、**ささいな問題ではない**。写真や動画、電子マネー取引なども含む話だ。**中国当局**は、そのようなデータを**諜報活動**や政治活動の監視に使用していることを隠していない。中国政府の監視の目がいったいどこまで届く可能性があるのかが、深刻な不安の種だ。残念ながら、データをローカライズすれば**リスクを回避**できるわけでもない。日本での最大のデータ**盗難事件**は、2014年に、通信教育事業などを行うベネッセホールディングスで起こった。1回のデータ漏洩で4,800万人が影響を受けた。

Data Security

Smartphone apps offer conveniences that many Japanese find highly attractive. One of the dominant communication tools has been the messaging service LINE, which has some 86 million domestic users. Even government ministries and local municipal governments have used LINE in their administrative services, including the reservations of slots for vaccines in 2021.

What the public did not know until March 2021 was that LINE Corporation had allowed a Chinese software company to access users' personal information. Personal information protection is important enough, but given China's National Intelligence Law (2017) and recent monitoring and surveillance of people around the globe—not just Chinese citizens—one would naturally worry if the Japanese government used LINE for transmission of data regarding national security.

The potential use of individual users' data is no minor issue. It includes photos, videos, and transactions of e-money. The Chinese authorities make no secret of their intention to use such data for state intelligence and monitoring of political activities. Just how long the reach of that government might be is a serious cause for concern. Unfortunately, the localization of data is not necessarily free of risks either. Japan's largest data theft to date occurred at correspondence education provider Benesse Holdings in 2014. This single data leak affected some 48 million individuals.

□利便性を提供する　offer convenience

□行政サービス　administrative service

□個人情報　personal information

□施行する　enact

□国家情報法　China's National Intelligence Law (2017)

□偵察行為　spying

□ささいな問題ではない　no minor issue

□中国当局　Chinese authorities

□諜報活動　intelligence activity

□リスクを回避できるわけでもない　not necessarily free of risks

□盗難事件　theft

45

❏ なぜ結婚するのか

生活・文化

Daily Life and Culture

日本の若者の中には引きこもりやオタクなどになる者もいるが、それとは別に、人生に満足している若者群がいる。彼らは実家に暮らし続けるので家賃を払う必要がない。彼らはファストファッション店で安く衣服を購入する。また今の世代は車を購入したいと思わず、代わりに時間に正確で本数も多い公共 交通機関を利用する。

ほとんどの場合、彼らは酒もそれほど飲まず、昔の同年代の人々ほどセックスもしない。彼氏・彼女を作ることにもあまり関心がなく、むしろ恋人がいると面倒だし、どのみち魅力的な相手があまりいないと言う。一人でいることを好まず、「特別な誰か」がいない代わりに、友人たちとリアルやネットで集うことを選ぶ。

彼らのような生活の負の面は、将来に何も期待していないので、今この瞬間を謳歌しようとすることだ。彼らには、上の世代の人々よりも安定的な職を見つけることが間違いなく難しい。年月がたてばたつほど終身雇用は少なくなるだろう。より多くの若者がパートや非正規雇用で長く働くことになる。

これは結婚や子育ての問題につながる。1970年には50歳まで一度も結婚したことのない人が人口の5%だったのに対して、2015年には人口の19%にまで増加した。これが自ら望んだことなのか、経済的な理由によるものなのかはわからない。

彼らが 志 を持たないのか、コロナ後を憂慮して単に日本経済に対して現実的な見方をしているのかはわからないが、彼らは小さなことに喜びを見いだしているように見える。インスタ映えする完璧なデザートを求めて奔走する姿はそのせいかもしれない。とあるコメンテーターが言ったように、彼らは本当に「さとり世代」なのかもしれない。

Why Get Married?

While some Japanese youth become *hikikomori* and others can be described as *otaku*, or nerds, there is another cohort of young people who find their lives rather comfortable. If they continue to live at home, they don't need to pay rent. They can purchase inexpensive clothes at low-cost brand stores. Since the current generation no longer hope to buy a car, public transportation is dependable and frequent.

In most cases, they drink less and have sex less than previous cohorts of their age. Few seem to be too concerned about finding and holding onto a boyfriend or girlfriend, saying having one would be troublesome and there aren't too many appealing candidates available anyway. Most would rather not be alone, but getting together with friends, in person or on social media, make up for not having a "special one" in their lives.

The potential downside of their lives is that they are enjoying the present moment because they see little to look forward to. They are certain to face less job security than earlier generations. Lifelong employment is becoming rarer as the years go by. Young people are more likely to end up working part-time or at non-permanent jobs for the long term.

This brings us to the issue of marriage and having children. Whereas in 1970 only 5% of the population was never married by the age of 50, in 2015 that figure had risen to 19%. Whether that is a choice or just a result of the economic realities they face is hard to judge.

Whether they lack ambition or are simply realistic about the economy of Japan, especially post-pandemic, some appear to seek happiness in small things. Perhaps that explains the search for the perfect dessert which is photogenic enough to post on Instagram. Perhaps they really are, as one commentator has put it, the *satori sedai*, the enlightened generation.

□〜群　cohort of

□実家　(one's parents') home

□ほとんどの場合　in most cases

□〜にはあまり関心がない　not have much concern for

□面倒　troublesome

□リアルやネットで　in person or on social media

□負の面　downside

□今この瞬間を謳歌する　enjoy the present moment

□上の世代　earlier generations

□終身雇用　lifelong employment

□憂慮する　be worried

□現実的な見方　realistic view

□インスタ映えする　Insta-worthy

□奔走する　run around

□さとり世代　Satori generation

46

森林浴
（しんりんよく）

オランダ語から英語に訳されたMaartje Willems と Lona Aalders作の『The Lost Art of Doing Nothing（何もしないという失われた芸術）』という書籍によると、オランダ人には独自の**リラックス法**があるという。それはniksen（ニクセン）と呼ばれ、意味は「**他の活動の不在**」だ。何もすることがなく、新たにすることを見つけないことを言うそうだ。予定していた活動をやめて、代わりに何もしないことで得られる状態でもある。

この2人の著者ですら、日本人には似たような**手法**があると言う。それは「森林浴」だ。**自分の心身の健全化**のために**自然に身を委ねる**ことを指し、通常ゆっくりと**心を鎮めて行う散歩**が含まれる。ハイキングではない。遠くには行かず、早く歩くわけでもない。この行為のコンセプトは、自分の五感を使って**自然を意識する**ことである。

森の中の散歩が体に良いのは当たり前ではあるが、自然を意識することでストレスを軽減し、**心拍数を低下させ**、血圧を下げる**生理学的効果**が得られるとの研究もある。元気を取り戻し、**仕事疲れ**を軽減してくれるかもしれない。

Forest Bathing

According to a book titled *The Lost Art of Doing Nothing*, by Maartje Willems and Lona Aalders, translated from the Dutch into English, the Dutch have a unique way of unwinding. It is called *niksen*, the "absence of any other activity." It is defined as having nothing to do and not finding something new to do. It can also be achieved by cancelling a planned activity and replacing it with nothing at all.

Even these two authors admit that the Japanese have a similar strategy. It is called shinrin-yoku, roughly translated as "forest bathing." It is the practice of immersing yourself in nature in order to improve your well-being. It usually involves a slow, mindful walk. Not a hike. You don't go far and you don't walk fast. The idea is that you contemplate nature with all of your senses.

Obviously a walk in the woods is good for you, but research in the physiological effects of this focusing on the beauties of nature suggests that it can lower stress, reduce heart rates, and decrease blood pressure. It may improve your energy level and release work fatigue.

□ リラックス法　relaxation method
□ 他の活動の不在　absence of any other activity
□ 手法　technique
□ 自分の心身の健全化　one's own physical and mental well-being
□ 自然に身を委ねる　immersing oneself in nature
□ 心を鎮める　calm one's mind
□ 散歩　walk
□ 自然を意識する　contemplate nature
□ 心拍数　heart rate
□ 血圧　blood pressure
□ 生理学的効果　physiological effect
□ 仕事疲れ　work fatigue

47

❏ 日本の価値観の利点と欠点

　日本の**伝統的価値観**やものの考え方には良い面がたくさんある。例えば、アメリカの文化とは大きく異なり、日本文化は**対立を好**まず、**他人への配慮を多**く見せる。「**遠慮**」を**推奨**すること——遠慮とは控えめ、自制、気配り、思慮深さを組み合わせたような**概念**だが——これは他の文化も何らかの形で取り入れてもいいように思う。

　特に「空気を読む」ことができるということは、**他人の視点により注意を払**うという意味で魅力的である。日本文化の肝とも言える調和を維持するのに必要不可欠な技術である。

　しかし、企業スキャンダルや**政治家の失言**、重大な災害が起こった時の**無責任体質**を見るにつけ、このような日本の伝統的な価値観にも欠点はあるような気がする。

　調和を求めるあまり、いつもとは言わないが、**画一性**に向かってしまうことがある。伝統的な**格言**に「**出る杭は打たれる**」というのがある。もしも個人が正当な意見を持っていたとしても、集団の中で**和を乱し**たくないからと**沈黙**してしまうと、何か価値のあるものが失われるかもしれない。結果、その集団全体が何かを失うかもしれない。全ての杭が飛び出ている方がいいのではないだろうか。いろいろな視点を議論して、合意を得る。これは**調和に取って代わ**る別の道である。

Advantages and Disadvantages of Japanese Values

There is a lot to be said for traditional Japanese values and ways of thinking. In sharp contrast with, for example, American culture, Japanese culture is less confrontational and shows more consideration of the other person. The promotion of *enryo*—a combination of reserve, constraint, tact, and thoughtfulness—is something that other cultures should consider adopting in some form.

Certainly the ability to "read the air," *kuki o yomu*, is appealing in that it pays more attention to the perspectives of other people. It is an essential skill in maintaining harmony, a key aspect in Japanese culture.

However, from observations of company scandals, public gaffes by government officials, and lack of a sense of responsibility when major disasters of various types occur, it seems there are downsides to these traditional Japanese virtues.

Efforts to achieve harmony sometimes—not always—lead to uniformity. The traditional expression says that the nail that sticks up gets hammered down. But if one person has a valid point to raise but remains silent out of a desire to go along with the group, something valuable may be lost. In fact, the whole group may lose something as a result. Would it not be better if all the nails stuck up? Discuss the different points of view and then work toward a consensus. That is another path to an alternative of harmony.

□ 伝統的価値観　traditional values
□ ものの考え方　ways of thinking
□ 対立を好まず　avoid conflict
□ 他人への配慮　consideration for others
□ 遠慮　a combination of reserve, constraint, tact, and thoughtfulness
□ 推奨　promotion
□ 控えめ　reserve
□ 自制　constraint
□ 気配り　tact
□ 思慮深さ　thoughtfulness
□ 概念　concept
□ 他人の視点　perspectives of other people
□ 注意を払う　pay attention
□ 肝　core, essence
□ 政治家の失言　political gaffe
□ 無責任体質　irresponsibility
□ 画一性　uniformity
□ 格言　proverb
□ 出る杭は打たれる　the nail that sticks up gets hammered down
□ 正当な意見　legitimate opinion
□ 和を乱す　disturb harmony
□ 沈黙する　remain silent
□ 調和に取って代わる別の道　another path to an alternative of harmony

謙虚さを表すために、企業の役員が会社のしでかしたことに対して全ての関係者に謝罪する風景は、メディアでもよく見かけられる。立ち上がり、謝罪をし、カメラマンを前に頭を深く下げて、再発の防止に向けて最善を尽くすと約束する。ほとんどの視聴者にとって、このような決まりきった風景は本当の謝罪ではなく、事態を改善する意志を感じさせるものではない。全て無意味なイベントである。

　裁判などで、責任ある地位にある者が部下の不祥事について知らなかったとか、災害は自らが想定できる範囲外であったと主張することは、他人への敬意を放棄することだ。彼らは誠意を欠き、自己中心的であり、謙虚で自責の念を持つことの正反対を行っている。

　このような状況では、一匹狼、出る杭、告発者など、全てを投げうって調和への流れに対抗しても良心に従う人々を、称賛したくなる。

　日本の伝統的価値観には高く評価されるべきものがたくさんある。しかし、この価値観の陰に隠れて他のことを考慮しないと、重大な問題を引き起こすかもしれないのだ。

Humility as displayed by company directors who apologize to all parties for something the company has done is a regular display in the media. Stand up, apologize, bow deeply for the photographers, and promise to make every effort to prevent a reoccurrence. To most viewers, these "set-piece" events are neither real apologies nor statements of a determination to do better. They are meaningless events.

When people in positions of authority claim in court cases that they were not aware of an underling's wrongdoing or that a disaster was beyond their ability to anticipate, they surrender the respect of others. They are insincere, self-centered, and the very opposite of humble and contrite.

On occasions like these, one wants to applaud the maverick, the nail that sticks up, the whistle-blower, and others with a conscience who are willing to go against the flow toward harmony at all costs.

The traditional values of Japanese culture have much to be admired. But hiding behind these values without other considerations can lead to serious problems.

□謙虚さ　humility
□会社のしでかしたこと　something the company has done
□謝罪する　apologize
□再発の防止　prevent a reoccurrence
□決まりきった風景　stereotypical scene
□不祥事　wrongdoing
□想定できる範囲外　beyond one's ability to anticipate
□誠意を欠く　insincere
□自己中心的　self-centered
□自責の念を持つ　have a sense of self-remorse
□一匹狼　maverick
□全てを投げうって　at all costs
□称賛する　applaud

Read Real NIHONGO

日本の論点
Japan Today and How It Got This Way

2024年2月3日　第1刷発行

著　者　　ジェームス・M・バーダマン

訳　者　　イヴォンヌ・チャング

発行者　　浦　晋亮

発行所　　IBCパブリッシング株式会社
　　　　　〒162-0804 東京都新宿区中里町29番3号　菱秀神楽坂ビル
　　　　　Tel. 03-3513-4511　Fax. 03-3513-4512
　　　　　www.ibcpub.co.jp

印刷所　　株式会社シナノパブリッシングプレス

© IBC Publishing, Inc. 2024

Printed in Japan

ISBN978-4-7946-0799-7